DISЯUPTED

From Gen Y to iGen:

Communicating with

the Next Generation

STEFAN POLLACK

with Noemi Pollack and Mark Havenner

Enjoy leArNiNg About iGen! Best [signature]

❖

Pacific Coast Creative Publishing
Los Angeles

1ST EDITION

Manufactured in the United States.

Published by Pacific Coast Creative Publishing, Los Angeles.

Jacket design by Bacall:Creative, © 2013.

ISBN-13: 978-0-9839641-5-5

Library of Congress Control Number: 2013930370

http://www.disruptedbook.com

Printed on acid free paper. Interior pages are Sustainable Forestry Initiative (SFI) certified. Meets all ANSI standards for archival quality paper.

Content Created in Association with:
The Pollack PR Marketing Group
Los Angeles | New York
http://www.ppmgcorp.com

Foreword

The book you hold in your hands is an important and timely book. Important because it deals with a major shift in generational characteristics that is altering the rules of marketing. Timely because there will soon be a generational shift in power almost unprecedented in human history.

The 20th century was when marketing and advertising truly came into its own, particularly in the second half when television became the dominant advertising medium. Companies created full-fledged marketing departments, retained ad agencies and developed brand strategies based upon delivering singular messages to mass audiences. Then things got complicated. The Internet arrived, connectivity soared, computing devices became ever more powerful, smaller and mobile. Technology disrupted marketing. Those in positions of power in the marketing understood this but, because of the legacy thinking they still held on to, they did not react fast enough. After all they came into the digital age as adults. They were, and may still be, immigrants to this new digital landscape.

Enter the iGen, a named coined by Stefan Pollack in this book. Stefan has uniquely defined them, and well. They were born after 1994. They have grown up entirely in the new digital age. While I use somewhat different names and dates for what I call the Shift Age Generations, the message is the same. iGen is the first generation to be born into the digital landscape. They can never remember there not being a computer in the home, mom and dad without cell phones, the Internet or all forms of content being available in digital devices. They are digital natives. They are the first generation to grow to maturity in the 21st century. This means that most of the rules and thinking from the 20th century about branding and marketing no longer work as they are of a time that has past. That is why this is an important book.

As a futurist it is very clear to me that the world is about to have a generation shift of influence that may well be unprecedented. First the Millennials and then iGen will, in just the next 10-15 years, ascend into the positions of influence now held by Baby Boomers and Gen-Xers. These new generations are more alike globally than they are like their elders. The Accelerating Electronic Connectedness I have written and spoken about for half a dozen years is enabling these young people to connect with each other globally in ways never before experienced. It is as though this ever-growing connectivity has created global generational tribes that have entirely different ways of communicating and using technology. They, not us, are defining how it will be used, what is accepted, and what is immediately rejected. Since they are the ascendant generations of our times, how they do what they do, think the way they do, embrace or reject and ridicule brands must be understood by brands and marketers.

Disrupted is a big step toward that understanding. So turn the page, or swipe the page on your screen and open your mind to the new world you must accept and embrace, if you want to remain an effective marketing or branding professional.

David Houle
Futurist
www.davidhoule.com

Introduction

Here we are, following one of the largest communication disruptions in human history, looking at the debris around us. The transformative nature of the decade of the millennium challenged much of what the last three generations had seen. The 'Boomers' had Vietnam, Kennedy, and the Cultural Revolution. Generation X had MTV, the AIDS crisis, and the Internet. "Generation Y/ Millennials" had September 11, social media, and the Great Recession. We have yet to see what "iGen" has. But we know the world they are moving into.

Every generation has its disruption; some more than others. For the Boomers, it was the cultural disruption. The upheaval of the neat and tidy world the postwar period brought for them and a vocal realignment of the values that stood in the face of their parents and the establishment. For Generation X, it was a knowledge disruption. The explosion of information that, in just a lifetime, tore down the Soviet Union and built a global society held on the shoulders of the Internet, 24-hour news, and cable television. For Generation Y, it was an economic disruption that converted laissez-faire access to information and technology into complacency, leading to recession, divisive political upheaval, and cultural ambiguity.

But with each generational disruption, there was an

equal and powerful generational innovation. The Boomers saw cultural innovation with civil rights, individualism, and government accountability. Generation X saw media innovation with popular culture, news and journalism, and exponentially escalating Internet technology. Generation Y saw social innovation with the power of consumers in social media and the rapid-fire spreading of ideas leading to global revolutions and systemic reversals of the roles of corporate, political, and economic power.

After the generational disruption, there is historically an aftermath and, ultimately, the "new normal." The Boomers lived in a world created by the disruption of World War II, where patriotic ideology reigned and the realities of the world around them were trapped in the confines of the Cold War. Generation X lived in a systematic dismantling of generational paradigms, leaving the world of the prior generation obsolete. Generation Y lived detached from the world, parsing the explosion of information into relevant bytes, easier to consume.

And what is the new normal for the next generation? Those that have already earned a few nicknames: Generation Z, the September 11 generation, the Digital Natives, Generation Next. For them, all that is known is post–September 11. There was always war in the Middle East. Mobile technology is a fact of life. Newspapers have always been obsolete. Television has always been served through computers. Consumers manage companies. Global news is relevant. There is omnipresent access to the Internet. Virtual identities are just as real as human beings. The online world and the real world are inescapably connected.

Those of us born in the three working generations of Boomer, X, and Y know what has happened in the past few years very well. However, it is time now to think about our children. For them, there is no other world. They are living in the post-disruption. While we are still trying to understand the new rules of the world, they are already intuitively navigating it. In just a few short years, this new generation will enter the workforce. They will buy products. They will consume media. They will be the future of our collective industries.

And why do we call this new generation iGen? Above

all, this is the mobile generation. This is the generation that will not be tied to a single location to consume products or information, whether it is a computer, a brick-and-mortar retail outlet, or a newspaper. This generation is growing up in a world with digital appendages, infinite touch points, and a permanent connection to the virtual world. This generation has unlimited knowledge at their fingertips and permanent access to any and all information that the whole of humanity possesses.

There is an implication that the term "iGen" credits the innovative company Apple with our most recent generational disruption. Certainly that point is arguable. Did the iPod, iPhone, and ultimately the iPad lead us into a new era, transcending all known levels of the information age? Or was Apple riding an already moving current that would inevitably lead to the technology that became so widely symbolic of the disruption? Time will tell. Brilliant minds for years to come will be working to find out the truth of that question. But one thing that is clear to the rest of us, whether Apple was the impetus for this disruption or whether it was the fortunate beneficiary of a larger trend, the iPhone and iPad were definitive conduits to causing a collision between the upward trending movements of social networking and the accessibility and bandwidth of wireless/cellular technology, resulting in a marketing free-for-all that fused the virtual and real worlds together.

It is apt, then, to coin the upcoming generation as products of symbolism embodied by Apple and its products. This should not discredit the other major players in the new marketplace, including Google, Amazon, Facebook, and other digital giants. But one thing we should consider is that Apple's vision was the impetus, and, because of its disruption, iGen will be forever defined by it.

iGen was born between 1994 and 2004 and is currently estimated to number around twenty-three million in the United States.[1] According to Howe and Strauss in their book *Generations: The History of America's Future, 1584 to 2069*,[2] the cyclical trends of generations predict that iGen will be largely "independent," as opposed to Gen Y's more "team player" nature. In the context of the great communication disruption of the latter part of this decade, the independent nature of iGen could manifest itself in what we refer to as a "war of relevance." iGen will only care about information if it is relevant to them, and, since the power of brand-engagement is in the hands of the consumer, they will serve as their own gatekeepers, awarding relevant information by sharing it with their trusted network of peers and burying irrelevant information so it will be invisible to their peers. This trend is already evident in early studies: 60 percent of iGen expects relevant advertisements, and 46 percent prefer funny advertisements.[3]

In addition to the war of relevance, the last decade's disruption resulted in the "mobile appendage." It is only partly true to call iGen digital natives; certainly they are, but the larger truth is that they are intuitively mobile. The use of mobile technology is now so engrained into the marketplace that children, preteens, and teens rarely perceive a world without connecting to it through a mobile device. More than half of children under eight have a mobile phone and more than a quarter of all parents have purchased mobile apps for their children to use.[4]

With this new mobile appendage, there is an unprecedented phenomenon. The consumer is now permanently connected and has seamlessly integrated the real world with his virtual world. Within this uncharted landscape is a tremendous opportunity to reach consumers on one of any of their infinite touch points. The opportunity, however, has a finite scope.

Given the enormous quantity of content, consumers are very sophisticated at filtering out who reaches them on their infinite touch points. And with this level of content control, the roles have reversed. Instead of the content creators informing the consumer what they should consume, the content- receivers are informing the creators what they should produce. The lucky few that are received well by iGen are proudly worn as badges before their peers, elevating the traditional effect of word-of-mouth marketing into a much larger and more vocal platform.

iGen holds the keys and will be calling the shots. Our success in the next era is contingent on our ability to communicate with the next generation. An additional ramification of this information overload is the need for efficient processing of information. Productivity is a measurement of success appropriate for the twentieth century; now it is the efficiency of managing information that will benchmark success. The infrastructure needed to support the global information explosion is also challenged. Bandwidth is already being consumed exponentially at such a pace that those in the telecommunications field fear it will one day become a scarce commodity only available to those who pay.

This generation joins Gen Y in claiming a majority of the world's population. Within a few short years, they will join Gen Y as consumers. This book will show both how digital natives have inverted the consumer/brand relationship, and how brands can thrive in this environment.

This is not a book about marketing or public relations. It is a book about relationships. The very definition of our industry has become obsolete in a short period of time. We must learn how to communicate with and embrace our new audience.

This is not a book about strategies and tactics. It is a thorough analysis of our new environment. We must explore this uncharted territory and chronicle our journey, taking note of each misstep, while drawing up an accurate map of how to reach our collective goals.

This is not a book about business. It is about people and the adults our children will become. Further, this is a book about the pitfalls and opportunities in our future.

This is a book about the opportunity we collectively have to recognize the dawn of a new normal, and then determine how to adapt and survive, or risk being left behind by a world so transformational and alien that all of our tried-and-true tactics will become impotent.

Ultimately, to understand iGen, we must understand ourselves.

This is a book about us.

Chapter One

"Apple Killed the Video Star" -- The Infinite Touch Point

On October 6, 2011, three year-old Bell repeatedly swipes her finger across a TV to change the channel.[5] Later, on October 14, 2011, French Internet activist Jean Louis's one-year-old daughter is confused and dismayed that the copy of *Marie Claire* magazine does not change images when her finger swipes across the page. Then, on October 25, 2011, three-year-old Jaden Lander, shouts, "Come on, iPad!" when an app featuring Sesame Street's Grover doesn't work properly.[6]

Amazing as it seems, even before kids can speak, they have the ability to operate mobile devices. Stories in the media have demonstrated that children understand the intuitive nature of the multi-touch system (largely introduced by Apple in its iPhone and iPad products) before they understand language.[7]

Further, more children are being exposed to this

technology more than ever before. It has been reported that more than 50 percent of children under eight have a mobile phone of their own.[8] Almost half of all affluent families have purchased apps for their children, and overall, a quarter of families have done so as well.[9]

What does it all mean? Plenty. It means that there was a disruptive change in information technology, and, while the mainstream tries to calculate what is going on, young people on the periphery of the mainstream are taking to it without any need for explanation or analysis. And it is that population that will be the mainstream tomorrow. Therefore, we should take note and figure it out.

This is a perfect storm. The storm could well have passed us by . . . if it wasn't for Steve Jobs.

On April 3, 2010, my staff and I were watching real-time reports on CNET, Mashable, and Twitter, while Apple introduced the iPad. As usual, the riveted crowd of techno influencers was overwhelmed, yet in the far reaches of the Internet, there were skeptics wondering if Jobs was needlessly creating a new product category, for it wasn't a phone and it wasn't a computer; it was something else entirely. And that something else fit the fledgling "tablet" marketplace, a traditionally failing market niche[10] and the type of risk Jobs always tended to avoid ever since he took the helm at Apple.

Yet there he was, presenting the Apple tablet. In the public relations world, we knew at this moment that we were witnessing one of the largest disruptions in recent memory.

What Apple managed to do on that spring day was more than just create a new product category. It went beyond just producing a sensationalized product with a remarkable design and style. What Apple did was fundamentally redefine how we look at communications. Even in its infancy, the iPad demonstrated that we are no longer tied to a computer, whether it is the desk supporting a desktop and cords, or a laptop with cords and equipment. The iPad, and the iPad 2 that followed it, simply made computers mobile. It created the environment for permanent connectivity and infinite touch points.

Still, even as late as 2012, other manufacturers have not caught up to the profitability and success of the iPad. "iPad killers" such as Kindle Fire, eReaders, and other tablets completely flopped in the fourth quarter of 2011.[11] And as late as June of 2012, Microsoft answered the market—to much acclaim—with its own Apple-challenging tablet: the Surface. Whether Apple's advantage is design, superior manufacturing, better marketing, or simply because Apple was the first to break the category isn't certain. But what is certain is that Apple has been riding the extended wave of disruption ever since that fateful day in April 2010.

Objective analysis will show that perhaps it wasn't the iPad that caused this disruption, but it certainly was the iPad that brought the disruption into the mainstream. The iPad wouldn't be possible if it wasn't for the perfect collision of technology that has occurred over the past ten years: smartphone technology, widespread cellular technology, satellite and GPS innovations, the maturing of the mobile service provider marketplace, increased cellular bandwidth, faster cellular data technology, high-speed Internet, etc.

But it was 3G technology that would give the iPad the cresting wave it needed. For the first time, such technology allowed easy mobile access to the Internet. Since 2000, wireless and mobile Internet technology innovated to the point where it became commonplace. As of 2010, more than 20 percent of the world's mobile phone users had access to 3G; data usage accounted for 90 percent of the traffic. Further, it is expected that mobile traffic will increase by 4,000 percent within the next two years.[12] It is only a matter of time before Internet use on mobile units will supersede Internet use on laptops or desktops. According to analyst Mary Meeker of Morgan Stanley, that time could be 2013. And with 50 percent of the media tablet marketplace and total revenue at 60 percent of the PC market, the iPad clearly dominates the marketplace and will continue to do so, until at least 2015.[13]

Apple is riding this mobile wave and continues to introduce innovations year after year: the iPad 2, the iPhone 4, and the iPhone 5. The new third-generation iPad was launched in early 2012.

Apple put a stake in the ground for the next generation to be mobile, and what is more, their very world-view would be fundamentally rooted in instant and infinite access to data, anywhere.

iGen is truly the generation Steve Jobs built.

While it would be a major disservice to downplay the impact of incredible innovators such as Facebook and Mark Zuckerberg, Twitter, Google and YouTube, Amazon and Netflix, these innovations were disruptive only in the industries they served. Apple's disruption impacted multiple industries and multiple generations. The shockwaves sent a volley of technological responses that have mostly seemed inadequate. While Android takes the mobile market share and Google reigns over the Internet, Amazon lords over ecommerce, and Facebook and Twitter innovate communication, it is Apple that propelled the disruption into the mainstream.

Now iGen lives in a world with digital appendages, permanent connectivity, and infinite touch points.

The disruption occurred because of a magical formula including the mainstream popularization of social media, innovative technology, and advancements in mobile and wireless technology. We may know why it occurred, but now we must understand how it affects those who don't know a world apart from the disruption. We must understand the implications of having infinite touch points as the new normal.

Changing Touch Points

Conventional wisdom in public relations and marketing says that a brand needs to interact with a consumer numerous times before they convert; that is to say, a product must favorably pass a person's consciousness several times before they buy it.[14] A company must be prepared to interface with a consumer throughout the buying cycle, whether it is during the research phase or the closing phase. And if it is not a product you are selling but an idea, you also have touch points to hit before your idea "sells."

It is debatable as to how many touch points are generally required before someone makes a purchase, but recently that number has surfaced as eight. In order to sell a widget through PR and marketing, a brand must interact with a consumer no less than eight times for them to actually purchase a product. That is why coordinated marketing programs that include public relations, advertising, and promotions are effective.

However, the scale of it is dramatically different.

It used to be that the only place one could "touch" a consumer was at a brick-and-mortar store, on television or radio, in print media, or, more recently, on a website or search engine. In all cases, the opportunities for touch points were finite. A consumer needed to have purchased a magazine, turned on a television, or sat at a computer in order for a brand to have access to them.

Things became even harder in recent years with recordable television. History's most effective and profitable touch point, the television commercial, fell on more deaf ears than ever before with the rise of DVRs. Suddenly, commercials were rendered useless with TiVo and other DVRs; another branding channel lost. Next, digital streaming jumped into the arena, and so even fewer commercials were being viewed.

If that wasn't enough, the very lucrative advertising industry in print media plummeted in a few short years, as readers exponentially defected to the much less lucrative online news channel. The industry lost $8 billion at the start of the recession of 2008 and continued to plummet thereafter.[15] Over three hundred newspapers closed in 2009 after a 30 percent decline in ad sales, and an additional 150 were shuttered in 2010.[16] A historically effective touch point was once again removed. Magazines suffered a similar fate at nearly four hundred down in 2009.

As such, during the great media disruption, companies and organizations found a significant decrease of effective touch points and a dramatic increase of ad avoidance. Consumers no longer needed to sit through commercials, flip over ads, or read editorial product reviews. They could now watch *Seinfeld* online, read their favorite articles on RSS feeds, and read product reviews on Amazon—all commercial free.

To brands living during the disruption, they saw the opportunity for touch points dwindle and sometimes disappear altogether, but the opportunity for touch points in non-traditional channels increased to such heights, it could be described as being infinite.

The Infinite Touch Point

The average American spends thirteen hours per week on the Internet, which is now equal to the amount of time they spend watching TV.[17] Five years ago, the average American spent six hours connected to the Internet. The difference? Now, *consumers take the Internet with them.* They are no longer limited to sitting in a chair to access the Internet, sitting on the sofa at home to watch television; they need not have access to a physical book to read, or go to the store to shop.

Now, they can be touched in every aspect of their life, whether they are at the museum, in the car, at the park, in school, skiing, at Disneyland . . . wherever. Whenever.

Organizations' *modus operandi* needs to change if they want to reach iGen.

The question is then raised, "How do I gain access to iGen's infinite touch points?"

First, it is about understanding the new marketing funnel.

Changing Marketing Funnel

With regard to consumer behavior, Baby Boomers, Gen X, and Gen Y all have the same assumptions in common. The marketing funnel model (also called the purchasing funnel), developed in the nineteenth century by E. St. Elmo Lewis, has been our *de facto* understanding for more than one hundred years. In short, the model states that a consumer undergoes the following journey with every purchase: awareness of the existence of a product/service, expression of interest in a product group, emoting desire for a particular brand or product, and finally taking action in purchasing the product.

Certainly this model has been adapted over time, but the principal concept remains the same: a general and open-ended decision-making process is narrowed down into a sales conversion through marketing tactics. If a brand is reaching the consumer throughout the funnel, then the consumer will naturally be led to making the brand's desired conversion.

The more modern version of the marketing funnel follows awareness to consideration, into preference, action, and finally, loyalty.

Next, the traditional tactic would be to intercept the consumer while he or she is considering and/or researching a product. It could be as simple as walking into a jewelry store to check out prices or looking up the blue book cost of a particular model car. If a brand does not touch the consumer at this point, there is no opportunity to move the consumer on to a desire for the product. A touch point here might be a sales rep approaching a shopper to answer questions, or an advertisement on a car-shopping site.

Once the research phase is over, the consumer will then "want" a particular brand or product. The next touch point would be to provide an imminent incentive to close the deal immediately, such as promotional giveaways, discounts, or free shipping. That last nudge tips the consumer into a conversion when he or she finally makes a purchase, and then is presumably happy, becoming loyal to the brand.

While not a spotless model, it is an effective one and

has been since the birth of marketing.

No longer.

With iGen, post-disruption, the funnel is no longer linear; it is cyclical.[18]

What happens in the post-disruption world is that the purchase funnel stays intact until post-purchase, when the process starts all over again. The key difference between the traditional system and the new system is that once the purchase is made, the consumer then enters the marketplace and, along with the company/brand, creates controlled information about the product that is then consumed by other potential consumers. Therefore, the brand no longer has control over the messaging and the brand isn't the only entity experiencing touch points with the consumer. Now consumers have touch points with other consumers.

iGeners now become aware of brands less through controlled brand messages and more through recommendations by their friends and peers, as well as through user-generated online content. Given our new user-created world, the influencer is now an information distributor.

Influencers behave like brands in almost every way but are separate and apart from them, creating additional funnels in the overall marketing funnel. The conglomeration of opinions and insights (touch points) from peers, friends, and other consumers are collected by these influencers and then *redistributed as controlled messaging back to the consumer.*

Brian Solis, well-known marketer and social media pioneer, aptly described this situation as a new version of marketing: one-to-one-to-many.[19] His assertion was that we are no longer in a world where the brand (one) funnels controlled messages to the consumer (many), but rather where the brand (one) funnels controlled messages to influencers (one), who then funnel subsidized controlled messaging to the consumer (many). This, in addition to the larger, much more complex funnel, adds peer and consumer touch points all along the brand's traditional pathway.

Forrester put a report together in 2007, just at the dawn of the global communication disruption of social media, calling attention to this phenomenon of an altered, and perhaps irreparable, marketing funnel model. In the report, it is made clear that not only has the funnel exploded into many different user-controlled funnels that reach consumers and influencers from many sources in addition to the brand, but also that the process was cyclical.

Any good marketer knows that the "loyalty" aspect of the funnel will result in word-of-mouth marketing that will generate a consumer-controlled funnel back into your marketing mix. However, Forrester points out that this is occurring at such an unprecedented scope, it really cannot be construed as a "phase" of the funnel but rather as the repeating of the process.

In short, touch points are just as critical at the point of conversion and thereafter as they are at the point of awareness. If loyalty is not converted into a one-to-one-to-many brand advocacy, then awareness will eventually disappear. The traditional funnel is so heavily eclipsed by the input of peers, consumers, and influencers, it cannot be heard amidst the noise.

iGen now has infinite touch points and, with the benefit of being always connected, must now filter all of those that are accessing him or her. Increasingly, the way to filter is to put trust into peers, friends, and other consumers. Therefore, it is more critical than ever to nurture the conversion and post-sale cycle in an environment that has become increasingly supported by word-of-mouth marketing.

Connecting the Dots

When trying to reach iGen, it is important to seek admittance to their infinite touch points. And once permitted, we gain access to them at any time and in any place. However, they don't let just anyone in; iGen is the bouncer to their own private club, and brands are standing outside, lined up down the street and behind a virtual velvet rope. If you look wrong, wear the wrong clothes, or say the wrong thing, you have to wait there and watch as better and cooler brands walk in.

There is a price of admittance to gain access to iGen. The new marketing model is full of many funnels, each with a competitive voice that iGen trusts and listens to more than marketers. To gain admittance, you must find ways to connect the pipes of all of the funnels so that iGen is routed through your channel, otherwise your voice will be drowned out through all the noise and conversation about your brand. iGen asserts a position of authority over brands more than any consumer has ever had before, and whatever the price of admittance, the cost for not being admitted is far higher.

- **Listen:** Learn iGen. Know them. Understand what they do and don't like. Become fluent in their language and memorize their habits. This need not require a million-dollar market research program; it simply requires that you listen. The good part about iGen is that they are open to those that listen to them, and they wear their habits on their sleeves. They advocate for good brand behavior by rewarding it with attention, likes, check-ins, and feedback. They live online, and while they may be private about their personal lives, they are very vocal consumers. You don't need to learn their demographics; you simply need to hear what they expect from you. And then deliver.

- **Converse:** iGen doesn't listen to broadcasting. If the message is not made specifically for them, it will fall on deaf ears. iGen expects personal attention throughout the purchasing process. They know they are their own gatekeepers, and for every thousand brands that blast messages around them, they will allow one brand through: the one that speaks specifically to them.

- **Deliver:** Upholding the brand promise is not a new idea, but with iGen, it is what will separate your brand from all of the others that use gimmicks to gain admittance to iGen's infinite touch points. You were allowed in because iGen believed what you told them. If you don't make that belief a reality, the consequences are worse than just losing a customer in the new model: you will lose an entire marketing funnel. iGen listens to each other, and so they can either be influential brand advocates or insurmountable gatekeepers.

Who

Starbucks

What Was Going On

In the fall of 2011, on the heels of the Great Recession, the economic environment was still as sour as a political divide, struggling to address the high unemployment rate. Starbucks, still thriving after the recession, decided to undergo a corporate responsibility program aimed at unemployment.

What They Did

Starbucks launched Create Jobs for USA, an online initiative created in collaboration with Opportunity Finance Network, whereby coffee drinkers could donate $5 toward loans for firms and organizations that would add jobs. In two weeks, the fund surpassed $1 million in donations. Starbucks seemed to excel in positive brand sentiment, far more than other job-oriented campaigns could.[20]

Why It Worked

Most corporate responsibility programs are done with the traditional marketing funnel, while Starbucks inversed it. Knowing that its customers are far more influential and effective than it is, the company (and CEO Howard Schultz in particular) pushed it out of the "institution's" hands, including Starbucks, Washington, DC, and corporate America, and into the hands of the consumer. Certainly, Starbucks put its money where its mouth was and donated $5 million to the cause, but the real impact came when its customers donated of their own volition. Inversing the marketing funnel created a much more widespread and effective impact, but in so doing, Starbucks extradited control to the consumer and let them do what they do best: consume.

Who

Taco Bell

What Was Going On

A lawsuit filed in Alabama in the early part of 2011 claimed that Taco Bell's beef was actually only 35 percent beef. The story took to the airwaves one late night and swarmed the media, creating relentless public conversation about their quality.

What They Did

Taco Bell launched an ad campaign that blitzed nationally, featuring a headline of "Thank you for suing us," then detailed the quality of its product. It fell short of having an impact, and so the company fell into a second wave of activity, whereby Taco Bell's employees advocated for the brand. Yet another tactic that fell on deaf ears.[21]

Why It Didn't Work

Taco Bell need only take a page from a similarly devastating incident that occurred at Domino's Pizza a year prior, when a video surfaced showing lewd antics of employees. Domino's responded with genuine apologies in social media and quantifiable measures it was taking to improve. The reason Taco Bell's approach didn't work was because the company was using the traditional marketing funnel. Advertisements are part of the machine that iGen does not listen to or take seriously. Taco Bell's second approach made more sense, had it opened up the forum of talk from only employees to Taco Bell customers. iGen doesn't listen to Taco Bell; they listen to people who eat (or don't eat) at Taco Bell. Putting the ball into the hands of the consumers in social media would have had more risk to the brand, but far more positive impact on the situation.

The Net Net

If you want your brand message heard, the message must come from consumers, not you.

Chapter Two

"Magazincs and Bubblegum" — The Omnipresent Impulse Zone

You are waiting in line to order your coffee, and while the six people in front of you are going through excruciatingly long orders, you happen to glance at a display next to you featuring a Bruce Springsteen collection you have never heard of. All you need to do to own the Boss's greatest hits is take the credit-card-sized iTunes card to the barista and gladly hand over your $9.99, plus the cost of the latte you ordered, then drive that "puppy" home, turn on your computer, log onto iTunes, type in a ten-digit code, download the album, and sync it with your iPhone! In just seven easy steps, you can be listening to *The River* and *Pink Cadillac*. But just think that only a few hours earlier, you had no idea that you even wanted to own it or hear it.

While it is certain your life is now more enriched, you may ask, 'Why in the world did I go through all of those steps when I could have just opened up iTunes from my iPhone and downloaded the album?' The answer is simple. It's for the same reason millions of people have bought magazines in grocery stores for more than fifty years when they could get a subscription for nickels on the dollar.

Impulse zones.

You had absolutely no idea you needed Bruce Springsteen until you saw his face on a display . . . in the impulse zone. That special place where we, as consumers, lose all of our inhibitions and simply "must have" whatever it is that is being presented. Magazines have been successful at this for decades, as have candy bars, gum, mints, and beverages. Impulse zones are the highest revenue-generating areas of any retailer and often have sales per square foot that by far surpass any other square-foot area in the store.[22] It is also the most competitive part of a store, usually costing marketers a pretty buck to place their product there.

The idea of the impulse zone is that shoppers who come in for milk and are waiting in line, presumably bored, suddenly see an interesting magazine cover or a candy bar. The customer did not come into the store with the intention of buying that magazine and, in fact, didn't even know that he or she *wanted* that magazine, yet because it was there right in between the customer and the cash register, the desire phase of the marketing funnel was invoked and an immediate conversion was made. Certainly there are promotional tools that can increase the potential for a customer to have the desire to purchase something in the impulse zone, but the net of it is that if it was not at the register, there would have been no awareness and consequently no desire or purchase.

The pioneer of impulse-zone marketing was *Reader's Digest*, who positioned their magazines at the cash register of grocery stores. The rest is history. Now, magazines and confections depend almost exclusively on sales at the "front end" or by cash registers.

Impulse zones have remained largely unaffected in the post-disruption world. Walgreens, arguably a baseline for retail trends, reported nearly a 7 percent increase in sales at the front end in 2011. That is a significant number, considering overall sales only went up 1.5 percent.[23] A research report by *Front-*

End Focus revealed that over 90 percent of shoppers will buy from impulse zones weekly and front-end sales alone account for an average of 1 percent of total store revenue.[24] That is a striking number when you consider the miniscule square feet assigned to the front end compared to the rest of the store.

Still, the effectiveness of impulse zones at retail front-ends could be questioned in light of the downturn in magazine sales of nearly 10 percent,[25] yet confections (impulse food items) were up almost 5 percent.[26] Analysis of this data may show several things, but with iGen in mind, the answer seems to materialize: impulse zones work, but people don't need to buy magazines at the front-end anymore.

Although clearly magazines, newspapers, and many other traditional communications channels are indisputably in heavy decline, that does not mean brands no longer have access to their readerships. On the contrary, they have access to an infinite number of touch points with their audience, because iGen is permanently connected and mobile. We recognize, however, that to get access to these infinite touch points, brands must understand the new marketing funnel and concede control of their brand message to consumers.

There is another way. Knowing that impulse shopping is still alive and well and that the impulse zone is continuing to be effective in the post-disruption world, we can then use the same tactics that marketers have been using for decades. The reason impulse zones are so alluring is because they skip the entire marketing funnel and appeal specifically to "desire" without awareness or research.

The same can be done in the online world. A major consequence of having infinite touch points is that there is now an omnipresent impulse zone.

One way for brands to gain access to iGen consumers is by paying the price of admittance. Another way is to skip the marketing funnel and appeal straight to the desire phase of the marketing funnel. Since the impulse zone is no longer limited to the front-end of retail locations, brands can tactically reach their audience simply by connecting the offline and online worlds.

Whispering in a Crowd

In the stone age of Internet marketing sometime around 2002, it became clear to those of us in public relations, marketing, and communications that it was conspicuous for brands to be absent online. Further, an online presence was a direct channel to a global audience that historically had been inaccessible. Like Kevin Costner's character Ray Kinsella, we tore down the profitable "cornfields" of traditional marketing in print and broadcast in order to build the "Field of Dreams" of Internet marketing, in the hopes that "they will come." But unlike the situation with Ray, every company with access to a modem also built a Field of Dreams, and so no one came, because no one knew where to go.

Enter SEO. The rise of search engine optimization as a marketing tactic really took fire around the middle part of the decade, just before the global social media disruption. Before Google completely redefined how the Internet was searched, indexed, and accessed, brands were left with no genuine way to get noticed apart from advertising. Google introduced a search algorithm that revolutionized the Internet because it organically brought forward results based upon how many other people linked to that result. Google's assumption was that it must be a relevant result if enough different people say that it is. Started in 1997, Google went public in 2004, and by 2010, the search engine received 72 percent of all US searches.[27]

By 2005 it became clear that if brands wanted to be found on the Internet, they needed to be found on Google; and if they needed to be found on Google, they needed to be "relevant" as defined by Google's mysterious algorithm. In just a few short years, a brand new industry was born, devoted entirely to making brands easily found on search engines in general and on Google in particular.

Those that adopted SEO practices rose up the search ranks quickly. Websites were optimized so that Google could find them easier and content could be published to incite links back to websites, further improving a website's position in the algorithm. Then, as social media began gaining popularity, the amount of relevant links back to a website could be compounded simply by participating in online communities. The benefits of good SEO were dramatic, long-lasting, and highly effective.

Sadly, those days are over. SEO is now commonplace in any online marketing plan, and the tools are so readily available that they are often incorporated into daily activities that almost anyone in a company can handle. SEO professionals have turned to churning out content optimized for search engines in order to take the labor away from brands, but their innovations are no more effective than what many companies do in their regular activity. Additionally, Google's algorithm is constantly adjusted, making tried-and-true tactics completely ineffective without warning.

To add to the SEO problem, Google's user interface has undergone very dramatic changes over the past couple of years. With the introduction of saved search histories, the ability to personally demote and eliminate search results, and the introduction of Google+ that, among other things, allows searchers to democratically choose the relevance of links, it is extremely difficult to apply "best practices" to SEO and still garner results.

And if that wasn't tricky enough, Google has worked hard on making the user experience easier and will automatically filter out results from the user; sometimes because they are redundant, contain misspellings, or even out of a physical geographic location. Results that were once hitting users never have a chance to come up amidst what Google considers to be more relevant results, determined not only by links to a website but also by the individual's personal browsing habits.

SEO, then, has been relegated to a tactic that, like all other standard tactics, is used by everyone who has an online presence. Therefore, to not use SEO practices means one falls completely out of view online. But conversely, since everyone is using it, one's voice is no different or louder than anyone else's.

Brands, especially those that have not been active online for more than five years, are now whispering in a crowd with little hope of reaching their target audience without an expensive and targeted ad campaign.

The War of Relevance has escalated in the search world so much that SEO is completely ineffective unless it is done as part of a holistic online marketing campaign that utilizes social media monitoring, engagement and marketing, advertising, online public relations programs, wire releases, online influencers, and a coordinated and consistent dissemination of content.

Increasingly, traffic sources are moving away from search engines altogether in favor of social sites and content sites. A recent study by Outbrain found that referrals to websites from social media took 11 percent and search took 41 percent. Content sites (such as news outlets) account for 31 percent of website referrals.[28] Certainly, search cannot be ignored, but increasingly, website traffic is directed from places other than search engines.

In the iGen age, this trend will be more pronounced. Increasingly dependent upon referrals from trusted sources such as content sites or peers, iGen will not need to use search engines as much and perhaps will only use it for specific queries. So once again, brands find themselves unable to get past the crowded space and have their whispers heard by the right audience.

Shouting in a Vacuum

The converse problem of "whispering in a crowd" is that no matter how impressive, important, or exciting your brand message is, you are not communicating with anyone. Facebook crested one billion users in 2012.[29] 1.2 billion people use the

Internet on their mobile phones.[30] 2.6 billion people use the Internet. So how is it that brands are speaking to no one when they are online?

iGen doesn't listen to brands; they listen to iGen. iGen already accounts for 18 percent of the world's population, or 1.2 billion, and is growing rapidly.[31] There are already seventy million members of iGen in the US alone.[32] iGen is a generation of digital natives who already know this landscape innately, therefore the vacuum that we see today will be even larger tomorrow. There aren't enough impressions that will reach these billions of Internet users. It isn't because the message is wrong, isn't targeted, or isn't effective. It is simply because no one is listening to it.

The Point of Desire

As discussed in the previous chapter, brands will only be listened to if they are given admission to iGen's infinite touch points. This will inevitably lead to a "War of Relevance," a topic discussed in a later chapter. For the purposes of the omnipresent impulse zone, however, it is important to know that while traditional tactics to "break through the noise" or "be heard" may be ineffective with the current and growing audience, the impulse zone still works.

For the impulse strategy to work, brands must tactically jump in at the point of consumer desire, completely circumnavigating the much more complex and harrowing marketing funnel of iGen.

Focusing on the omnipresent impulse zone is especially important simply because the brand is no longer in control of the consideration/research phase. To iGen, that phase belongs almost exclusively to peers, friends, and other consumers.

The impulse zone doesn't need awareness, consideration, or research. It doesn't even need loyalty. It simply needs to be there. That is the biggest advantage brands have in this new infinite touch point reality. The most effective and visible touch point with a consumer is through the omnipresent impulse zone.

If brands can reach a consumer right at the moment they are going to make a purchase (or convert), then the complicated mess that was once the marketing funnel can be avoided altogether. This cannot be accomplished through traditional channels such as media relations, advertising, or e-mail marketing, unless that brand has been given admittance to iGen's infinite touch points, because those tactics are among the noise of other content creators and are ignored if not relevant. Additionally, even though the impulse zone in this new, permanently connected world is omnipresent, it is still *physical*; in other words, it is physically in the location of the consumer. Impulse zones only work if the consumer is (a) present and (b) about to make a purchase.

Then how does this translate into the permanently connected world of iGen, who opt to purchase books at Amazon and download to a Kindle rather than visit a bookstore; download music to an iPhone instead of visiting a music store; and purchase clothes and furniture on eBay instead of going to the mall? The problem with having an omnipresent impulse zone is that there is no one *physical* location to reach the consumer. But like infinite touch points, once you have managed to access the omnipresent impulse zone, you have direct access to the consumer at the point of purchase.

Fortunately, there is a massive upward trend that consists of entirely fusing the offline and online worlds together.

The Check-In Revolution

In 2007, the iPhone's launch quickly fanned the flames of an already ripening app-development market. The marketplace for "check-ins" was crowded by this time with Brightkite, Loopt, and Foursquare's predecessor, Dodgeball. When it was re-tooled for iOS, the explosion began.[33]

Foursquare's magical formula for gamifying check-ins catapulted them to the lead of the highly competitive location space. By awarding badges and mayorships, Foursquare cultivated social competition and fed psychological awards to keep consumers active. Many other contenders fought for market share, including Gowalla and smaller start-ups, leading to what many in the tech field called "check-in fatigue" as consumers decided what service to use.

Facebook blew the lid off the channel by introducing "places" in late 2010, which allowed Facebook users to check in—a direct affront to leading rivals Foursquare and Gowalla.[34] Since then, Facebook took a massive market share from Foursquare by hanging its hat on natural integration with existing Facebook services. Foursquare continued to grow by 100 percent and so Facebook killed "places" in favor of allowing check-ins with status updates. With the 2012 introduction of its "Timeline," the location-based check-in then became much more interactive and useful, allowing Facebook to further dig its heels into Foursquare.[35]

It is too early to tell which of the location-based services will reign supreme, but Foursquare is still the classic standby and Facebook is very much a contender. What happened to Gowalla? Some people probably still use it. However, this multi-year war for location-based service supremacy has demonstrated something quite profound: iGen likes to check-in and that trend is here to stay.

On the surface, critics may argue that the "check-in" cannot seriously kick up dust as a digital trend, because who cares where you are physically located when interacting on the Internet? In the heat of the location-based services war, at the first part of 2011 a study by the Pew Research Center demonstrated that only 4 percent of smartphone users "check in."[36] By the end of 2012, however, that number went up by 32 percent.[37] Now with Timeline and check-in deals through Facebook, it is expected this trend will continue to climb.

The reason for this increase isn't necessarily, as critics suggest, because check-in users are simply bragging about where they are to show off to their network, nor is the trend a superficial bubble that will inevitably burst, making "2011: The Year the Check-In Died," as ReadWriteWeb continued to state. Interestingly, ReadWriteWeb's article[38] moves on to discuss the very tactics that are causing the check-in trend to persist to today. By allowing photos, tapping into deals, and making the activity more social, the check-in has become the "like button" of the real world.

This is a major and very recent development that will likely cement the check-in as a constant tool for iGen. The generation has been trained from birth to declare their organizational affiliations publicly, both to demonstrate their lifestyle and also to plug into a like-minded community. The check-in allows them to do this in the real world too, effectively fusing their online and offline personas.

In the context of the omnipresent impulse zone, the task for brands is to *virtually* reach iGen in the real world using location-based services.

One of the simplest ways to do this is to use an age-old impulse-zone tactic: deals.

Geo-Location Offers

LivingSocial and Groupon have been extraordinarily successful in this new environment for one reason: they capitalize on the infinite touch zone. Consumers have a specific need (massage, dinner for two, movies, car mechanic, etc.), they have a purchase channel (Groupon, LivingSocial), and an impulse zone ($20 off, free dinner). It is physically tied to their location and in a channel they were already using.

There is a more fundamental movement at play here, however. The most effective uses of the omnipresent impulse zone are tactics that leverage the marriage of the physical and virtual worlds. Improved geo-location and GPS technology, augmented reality, and innovative mobile applications have blurred the lines between the virtual world and the real world. Apps in production now superimpose information and images over the physical world when viewed through the phone. Still others create games in a virtual setting using real-world locations.

Although in a feeble upward trend in the US (but much more prevalent in Asia), special bar codes, called QR codes, can instantly direct a mobile device to any online location and result in impulse zone, driving conversions as well. When this trend truly catches on, consumers will be able to connect to any virtual location by interacting with a physical object. It is Hollywood and video game makers who have pioneered this tactic and who provide special "Easter eggs" of information for consumers who take the time to scan the bar codes on movie posters.

As technology improves, there will be a virtual overlay on top of the real world that will tell iGen everything he or she wants to know about the brand. The overlay already exists; it is only a question of which interface can best access it.

Connecting the Dots

- **Check-In:** iGen uses the check-in as a like button for the real world, therefore it is important for a brand to cultivate this behavior by being likable in the physical world. Incentivizing impulse check-ins advocates for a brand to iGen's personal network and can, in many cases, serve as a shortcut to gaining admittance to iGen's infinite touch points. By checking-in, iGen is wearing the brand as a badge, informing his or her peers that the brand is worth interacting with and is trustworthy. Check-ins, therefore, are a critical way to leverage the impulse zone, gain consumer advocacy, and then access iGen's touch points.

- **Convert:** The beauty of an impulse zone is that one need not go through the traditional marketing funnel in order to make a sale. This is a tremendous opportunity that can be leveraged through discounts and promotions. Utilizing location-based services like Groupon and LivingSocial gives direct access to an omnipresent impulse zone and can effectively cut through the clutter of having to use a marketing funnel to reach a consumer.

- **Fuse:** Ultimately, accessing the omnipresent impulse zone means fusing the offline and online worlds. Any physical location that can connect to the virtual world and vice versa can serve as a touch point for your brand. Placing these offline and online "locations" at the point of purchase puts the touch point in the impulse zone; this is true whether in a geo-location deals app or on a placard on a retailer's front-end hosting a QR code with a discount attached.

Who

Apple and Starbucks

What Was Going On

Apple saw tremendous success by 2007 with its iTunes format, the iPod, and then its iPhone. iTunes was likely a major player in solidifying the demise of the physical record store. Yet the interaction with consumers was entirely in the online world. Apple, rather intelligent when it came to retail marketing, needed a way to fuse the offline and online worlds and access a physical real-world channel for its consumers.

What They Did

It occurred to both Apple and Starbucks that they largely serve the same clientele. So they brought the virtual world into the real world using, arguably, the country's most coveted impulse zone: the Starbucks front end. Apple and Starbucks launched a "pick of the week" program, offering free iTunes songs on cards at the cash register. The partnership proved successful, and now there are gift cards of all types of products in most retail locations.

Why It Worked

Apple and Starbucks simply did what retailers do best: put a product in the impulse zone. The difference was that this product was a digital one. It opened a new distribution channel previously not widely used. The execution of this partnership demonstrates how one can effectively reach iGen by circumnavigating the marketing funnel and reaching them at the point of purchase, even with a digital product.

Who

Borders, Tower Records, Blockbuster, etc.

What Was Going On

With the popularization of MP3s and MP3 players, namely the iPod, record store sales went into a sharp decline at the start of the decade. Widely symbolized by the fall of Tower Records in 2004, the industry lost hundreds of millions of dollars over the course of a couple of years.[39] After the dust settled, it was clear that the big-box stores like Best Buy and Wal-Mart would be the only brick-and-mortar players in the industry. Netflix was born, and, within six years, it killed the massive and previously unmovable Blockbuster chain. Then, in the latter part of the decade, the iPad, Kindle, and Nook delivered crushing blows to brick-and-mortar bookstores, ultimately leaving Borders bankrupt and Barnes & Noble sales in sharp decline.

What They Did

The record industry, the video industry, and now the book industry, have all fallen victim to the new disrupted environment where consumers don't need to leave the virtual world to consume. Accessing MP3s was as easy as a click. Video stores were necessary evils for many; browsing the store, standing in line, and getting the tape or disc back at odd times the following day to avoid a late fee. Now, they are streamed on a computer or tablet. Now the publishing industry is facing the same crisis, as Amazon takes the lion's share of the marketplace and e-book sales soar by more than 300 percent, with e-readers becoming the de facto interface for reading.

Why It Didn't Work

The failing brick-and-mortar enterprises were sucker-punched by innovations during the first decade of this millennium, and they could not adapt their antiquated processes quickly enough. Barnes & Noble took on Amazon with the Nook, however that effort is also losing steam as the company announced they will no longer be making Nook tablets, but rather support software on other tablets.

The Net Net

Find a consumer's point of purchase in both the virtual world and physical world and then meet them there.

Chapter Three

"And You Are...? And This is Regarding...?" --
The War of Relevance

Comedian David Spade's finest performance was, arguably, the bullet-proof and holier-than-thou receptionist to Dick Clark that he played on *Saturday Night Live*. No one could get past his eye-rolling snotty presence, no matter how important or well known they were. He would indiscriminately ask, "And you are?" No matter if the person was Roseanne Barr, MC Hammer, or an alien from outer space.

iGen is David Spade's Dick Clark receptionist. There is no positive or negative discrimination for brands; there is only the question (often unspoken), "Who are you and what do you want?" If the answers to either of those questions are wrong, iGen will subsequently ignore you. In this metaphor, it is probably truer to say iGen is Dick Clark Productions and they serve as their own David Spade receptionist. They have a wall put up against brands, and they only allow through those who are loyal and bend their knee in fealty. The others have to wait outside the castle walls and throw ineffective branded messages against it.

We know that iGen doesn't listen to brands; they listen to iGen. We also know that it takes admittance to reach iGen's infinite touch points and the cost of admittance is surrendering the brand from controlled messaging to consumer-to-consumer messaging. Additionally, we know that iGen is just as receptive to impulse marketing as the other living generations, but that it must be achieved through the omnipresent impulse zone by fusing the offline and online worlds at the point of purchase. But what of traditional marketing, public relations, and advertising? If this is all true, is there a place at all for controlled messaging?

The tools of marketing have, by and large, remained the same, but their effectiveness on reaching the audiences has changed. Ad avoidance is increasing tremendously and the media audience has dwindled. So advertising is relying upon interactivity more than on controlled and persistent messaging, while public relations is relying less upon the media to relay messages to the consumer and more upon reaching the consumer directly through targeted programming. Yet there is still a fundamental need to broadcast controlled messages to audiences. In the new disrupted environment, however, controlled messages are in a "War of Relevance," and it takes strategic insight into the audience in order for a message to survive the battles of this war.

The "Look-It-Up" Generation

In the last chapter we discussed two problems: "whispering in a crowd" and "shouting in a vacuum." The information age has evolved to the point where there is virtually no cost associated with producing and receiving information. Therefore, the abundance and accessibility of information is infinite and instantaneous. According to some organizations such as the Internet Society, free and public access to information is a fundamental human right,[40] and the primary vehicle to accessing information is the Internet.

Therefore, one must look at technology trends to learn how such ready and instant access to information has changed us or, in the context of marketing, how it affects our behavior. One recent study conducted by UCLA found that children "digitally hard-wired since toddlerhood" are perhaps rewiring their brain circuitry, causing decreased social skills.[41] Another study suggests that "deep reading" comprehension may be achieved via a new hardwired shortcut, allowing earlier and more instant reading comprehension. The same UCLA study demonstrated that iGen and Gen Y display faster decision-making skills, and, ultimately, they could process information far more quickly than non-digital natives.[42] This study made some noise in that scientists are concerned we are losing our ability to socially connect face-to-face. However, from a marketing point of view, that may be a subsequent point.

The larger point is perhaps that technology is making us smarter. One takeaway from the study was that Internet users are very effective in processing information through searches; in other words, looking stuff up. And why shouldn't we be? Our brains no longer have to store data. We can look up anything, anywhere. We don't need to remember phone numbers, addresses, historical dates, shopping lists, or even birthdays. All information *relevant* to us is available at the push of a button. If the human brain is anything like a computer, it could be said that we are no longer storing anything on our hard drives, so therefore we have freed up our brains to process more information. Since we are not weighed down with data, we can process much more quickly and much more efficiently.

How else are we able to live in an environment with seemingly endless amounts of instantaneously accessed information? We simply trust our data systems to store it, and instead of remembering the data, *we remember how to access it*. Therefore, our ability to connect seemingly unrelated pieces of data or cognitively process information has exponentially improved. No longer burdened with recalling information, we simply need to connect the dots of all the information that is stored for us on electronic devices.

Humans have always been good at storing and archiving data. However, now we are so efficient at storing and archiving data that we no longer have to *learn it*. We can simply look up information and move on. Critics, particularly in the education system, have seen a lack of capacity for critical thought with digital natives; that is, the inability to effectively create actions that result in desired outcomes or to intuitively navigate scenarios with which they have no experience.[43] This is likely due to the fact that iGen and Gen Y never had to use critical thought in their academic lives because everything could be looked up. In prior generations, one couldn't simply find the answer to some problems and one would have to earn the information through critical thought or memorization.

Comedian Pete Holmes recently addressed this in a hilariously philosophical rant about how Google is ruining our lives. His well-put point was that we "know everything," but we are "not a lick smarter for it." And further: "The time between not knowing and knowing is so brief that knowing feels exactly like not knowing."[44] His rant escalates into how that time in between not knowing and knowing is usually filled with things like finding one's life partner. The larger point, however, is that knowledge used to be earned, but now it is simply accessed.

Clearly there is a downside to our new environment. If critical thinking skills, social skills, and human experiences become trivialized, then the cost could be too high. However, we could be going through a growing phase, where post-disruption settles into a "new normal" whereby we, as a species, are more intelligent and are able to process information more quickly and reliably than ever before.

Time will tell. However, what we do know is that Gen Y was the first of the digital natives and, while they process information differently than prior generations, iGen is exponentially different. Members of iGen are also digital natives but, more importantly, they exist in post-disruption in a world no longer limited by physical boundaries. Their capacity to connect dots, process information, and multitask will so transcend prior generations that they will have a much higher capacity for acquiring knowledge.

Using the old tools on iGen, then, will be largely ineffective. The old tools assume a process of sorts that guides consumers through a channel of understanding. For example, a product is introduced through the traditional media, advocated by reviewers, and described by marketing copy. A consumer is introduced to a product, is encouraged to gain trust in buying the product, and then learns about it. With iGen, they will have figured out what the product is long before the media is introducing it, they will already have decided whether or not their peers advocate for the product, and they will have ignored any marketing copy distributed to them.

They will have looked it up, connected the appropriate dots, and made a decision entirely without a brand's input. Therefore, to integrate into iGen's decision-making process, a brand must be relevant to them.

Features + Benefits ≠ Value

When discussing the War of Relevance, we are really looking at two similar but different concepts. There is a War of Relevance that happens on the surface, whereby brands compete with other brands to be relevant to their target audience, but then there is the deeper and more impactful War of Relevance, whereby brands work to become *necessary* to the audience. The first war is skin-deep and short-term; the second is long-term and fundamentally more effective. To be relevant to a target audience in the war against other brands, a brand's weapons are features and benefits, but in the war to become necessary to the consumer, the brand's weapon is value. Features and benefits only take a victor so far; the War of Relevance is truly won when a brand effectively communicates its value.

The importance of brand value is not new, nor is it any less important when talking to iGen. The difference between yesterday and the post-disrupted world is that communicating only features and benefits is a fast way to get ignored. iGen isn't interested in what a brand *does*; iGen is interested in what a brand *does for iGen*. The reward for winning over iGen by communicating value is that iGen will advocate for the brand and will even wear it as a *lifestyle badge*. However, if a brand is only communicating options, price, function, or any other feature/benefit, iGen will not only prefer other brands that demonstrate value, but will also not even hear the brand's messages.

Before iGen, being relevant was often a discussion of features and benefits, but it was positioned so that the audience would "notice" or "care." For instance, take a beer that both tastes great and is less filling. If you put those features in a commercial along with scantily clad women on the beach, then you are "selling" those features to a particular audience. Another example: having cheap car insurance is a feature, and using an animated gecko to explain that feature in a commercial is targeting this feature to a particular audience.

iGen doesn't receive messages in this way very well. A recent study showed that iGen and Gen Y prefer advertisements that "are relevant" to them and/or "are funny." Without getting too psychological, it can be gleaned that relevance is important and the reason "funny" is important is that it makes the ad more relevant.

Take, for example, Old Spice. A wildly popular Super Bowl campaign catapulted Isaiah Mustafa to stardom, as he humorously played on machismo. Strutting through "masculine" activities while eloquently persuading women to encourage their men to use Old Spice body wash, did not use one drop of feature/benefit messaging. The commercials were not telling audiences that Old Spice was cheaper, cleaner, or even that it smelled better than any other body wash. The commercial advertised a *value*, not a feature. It advertised the idea that if men use this product, they will be masculine and women will like them. Of course, it was tongue-in-cheek, but the value statement stood.

In a similar campaign, Dos Equis avoided the "tastes great, less filling" approach to marketing its beer by running through the incredible feats of "The Most Interesting Man in the World," who at the end of each commercial doesn't say to drink Dos Equis and be like him, but instead says that he *doesn't always drink beer*, but when he does, he *prefers* Dos Equis. The value statement is clear: Dos Equis makes you desirable, intelligent, and... awesome. What does it taste like? Who cares?

Further, value statements cannot be contested. A feature or benefit can be: Brand X toilet paper is 20 percent softer (really?); how about Brand X toilet paper makes your life comfortable (say, I like comfort!).

Successful value statements are everywhere in marketing: Snickers satisfies, Just Do It, Think Different... even McDonald's doesn't talk about how their food tastes (or that it is inexpensive): I'm loving it. These messages resonate with audiences. Price point, ingredients, the needs fulfilled are all subsequent to how the person can identify with a brand.

Marketing and communications often work hard to get something "noticed." It does no good to have something noticed only for it to be completely discarded after that. Communicating based upon value prevents a "features/benefits" war with competitors, bypassing them with a message that either identifies with the audience, or doesn't. When iGen advocates for a brand, they have to find value with it, identifying with the brand. That happens when the brand is made relevant to them.

iGen Connects Dots

Above the surface level of "being relevant," brands must genuinely integrate into iGen's lifestyle to become truly relevant. Relevance in the post-disrupted world is less about appealing to the ego of the audience and more about being an integral piece of their daily lives. Brands need to be needed by iGen.

If studies and anecdotal evidence are to be believed, iGen is highly adept at multitasking. As discussed earlier, to multitask, one must abandon storing information and learn to process where information is located (i.e., look things up instead of memorize). Since the tools available today are trustworthy storage devices, iGen will not be raised to store data and information; they will be trained from birth to reference data and draw conclusions.

We are already at a point where average people, no matter the generation, no longer memorize phone numbers or birthdays. Our devices are so good at storing this data and alerting us when we need it, we no longer have to waste brainpower on these types of processes. Psychologists say that since we don't need to remember anymore, it frees up the brain to do other things, ultimately making one more "intelligent."[45] So it becomes less about knowing something and more about knowing *where to find* information about something. That is why iGen is so good at multitasking; the source of their intelligence is directly related to the fact they have to process multiple avenues at the same time in order to obtain information.

This new mode of thinking is impacting almost every aspect of iGen's lives. The largely linear educational system is failing to achieve results with younger students because their attention spans cannot be held. Studies show that not only iGen has shorter attention spans, but also Internet users in general do.[46] Studies also show that students are much quicker to achieve understanding of topics when left to their own devices (or the Internet). One recent study demonstrated that students learn better in an online environment than in a classroom. If this is the case, it is no wonder educators are reporting increased boredom and shorter attention spans from their students. Chances are, they are figuring out the "point" of the lessons way before the information has been disseminated through lectures and assignments.

This is parallel to the marketing problem. Long before marketers get a message out, iGen has already formed an opinion about that message. iGen is very good at "connecting the dots" or finding seemingly irrelevant pieces of information and coming up with their own conclusions. This ability to multitask allows iGen to touch and process incredible amounts of information concurrently, and so referencing, cross-referencing, and acquiring pertinent data in a moment's notice comes naturally to them.

That being the case, if iGen is interested in making a purchase, chances are they have already looked up your brand, figured out whether or not it fits in their marketing funnel, and decided whether or not they will purchase it without having once entertained a single word of your messaging. To compound the issue, this process happens in real time, while iGen is mobile and generally sharing, again in real time, with iGen's entire network of peers and other consumers.

The challenge for relevance then is not about appealing to iGen through creative messaging that will remain unseen or ignored, but about *becoming one of the dots* that iGen connects with. In other words, brands must be ingrained into iGen's thought processes continuously and in real time. This is done not through-controlled messages, but rather by being a *necessary ingredient* to iGen's decision-making.

Being Necessary, Not Noticed

Success in the War of Relevance means being the inevitable solution to a problem they are working out, or a necessary topic in a conversation iGen is having, or a required step on the way to finding the answer to a question.

Brands must be one of the dots that iGen connects naturally. Strategically, this will mean a de-emphasis on content *creation* and an emphasis on content *curation*.

Arguably, the most important part of the marketing funnel is research/consideration. Consumers are aware there is a brand called Ford, but they need to know things like gas mileage, safety ratings, factory-installed sound systems, etc. In the old model, Ford would have to put a tremendous amount of effort into creating content about their cars to consumers, designed to reach them in the consideration phase through public relations, advertising, and promotions. If Ford was not doing that, then Honda was, and so Ford would lose its market share.

However, in the post-disrupted world, there is no shortage of information on Ford cars put out by consumers. There is far more content created than Ford could ever produce, and Ford has no control over this information. That doesn't mean that Ford is invisible to the consumer, but it means their content isn't valued as much as it was. In this new model, Ford has to accept that creating content is no longer the key to turning a considering customer into a buying customer.

Enter Scott Monty. On the eve of the social media explosion in 2007–2008, Scott Monty very early on became the poster child for how brands can and should operate in this new space. His direct and often witty approach to interacting with consumers in their territory demonstrated a genuine interest in the individual consumer and, in many ways, validated the idea that the consumer was now in charge of the marketing funnel.

Scott and his team changed Ford's role from content creation to content curation. Instead of producing new content, Scott collected relevant content and redistributed it to the consumer. So now Ford wasn't speaking with Ford's voice; it was speaking with the *collective voice of other consumers*. In the post-disruption world, consumers don't listen to brands; they listen to other consumers. Now consumers listen to Ford because they aren't speaking; they are curating the voices of other consumers.

Sure, Scott Monty puts out Ford messaging in a controlled way on Twitter, but the larger point is that a *person* is on

Twitter, implicitly inviting any, and all consumers, to say anything that they want. The very process of interacting on Twitter curates a funnel of consumer conversations, and Scott/Ford is in the center of that conversation, moderating it, contributing to it, and, ultimately, controlling it.

Curating content means implied objectivity about who you are and what you are offering. There is no attempt to "sell" when you are collecting valuable information and offering it to people who are looking for it. It also creates a thought leadership platform whereby a brand positions itself as both an expert and a source of information. Becoming skilled curators of information gives consumers a reason to listen to your brand. You are providing valuable information that they want, and you are helping them connect their dots.

There is more need for curation today than there ever was. With media in its massive disruption and the decreasing news audiences, coupled with the increasing direct-to-consumer interaction, many brands bypass the media altogether. Just because media circulation is decreasing, it doesn't mean consumers don't want the information anymore. Therefore, they are increasingly turning to brands that curate information to find consumer-oriented news.

Some brands have already caught on to the importance of being curators and newsmakers. These brands have realized that iGen can be reached by providing information about related topics without promoting themselves. One leader in this strategy is Cisco, who created a news site where they curate content from all over the tech world and from actual journalists, creating a news source that appeals to anyone searching for tech information.

Creating the news is still important, but until brands have earned the trust of iGen, the news will not be valued. So it is increasingly important to curate news that iGen is seeking out so that when the time comes that you do need to create the news, there is already a built-in audience of willing listeners.

The War of Relevance is won when iGen goes to you for knowledge, not just data. Anyone can produce content, lists of features, or controlled messages. But the brands that will thrive with iGen will understand that information must be cultivated and turned into knowledge that is useful for the audience. Curating information relevant to a brand but not necessarily created by the brand will create more "dots" for iGen to connect when they are searching for relevant information. If a brand connects enough dots with the consumer, then trust will be earned and the reward will be access to the consumer's infinite touch points.

Who

American Express

What Was Going On

American Express, while certainly ingrained in the business world, was still considered a credit card. In 2007, the company decided to start a branded thought leadership platform where it could allow business leaders to discuss business, housed under the AMEX brand. It was one of the earliest brand journalism exercises launched.

What They Did

Beginning in 2008, AMEX had seven big-name small-business writers, and by 2011, the site hosted over two hundred contributors, with over ten million page views and has become a respectable source of business insights, strategies, and news.

Why It Worked

American Express is a very well-known brand, but before Open Forum, it was not considered a business thought leader. By creating a forum for other business leaders to speak, their halo effect transitioned public perspective of the brand, and now, due to engaging curation, AMEX is a valued source for businesses.

Who

Traditional Advertising

What Was Going On

Even before social media and the great disruption of mobile and tablet technology, advertising had reached a nearly improbable pinnacle of clutter. It was increasingly difficult for a single message to break from the clutter of other messages and "be heard" by a target audience. As early as 2009, ad-avoidance was nearing 50 percent,[47] and by 2011, it was over 60 percent. And while certain online video ads ranked very well on ad avoidance, traditional media did not.

What They Did

Interestingly, the IPG study[48] demonstrated that it was not DVRs that caused ad-avoidance, but rather mobile phones and tablets. In the past few years, TV was focused on DVRs as a problem and newspapers on online news. The real problem was that consumers were becoming mobile and permanently connected, and so were increasingly distracted from traditional media.

Why It Didn't Work

Traditional media still assumes a linear funnel of access. It was thought that DVRs were causing ad avoidance because it was assumed the consumer was doing nothing but watching TV. The reason traditional ads could not keep up the pace was because they were not on a mobile device and therefore were not relevant to the consumer's experience.

The Net Net

Creating relevance for iGen is about becoming valuable to their decision-making process.

Chapter Four

"The Cool Kids" Influencing the Influencers

Perhaps the greatest challenge with reaching iGen is that iGen has grown from birth to ignore messages from brands, unless those brands have earned admittance to their infinite touch points. Instead of controlled messages from brands, iGen listens to their trusted network. iGen will check out Amazon comments, ask about products on Twitter, or pose a question on Facebook before making a buying decision. These kinds of activities do not typically allow for brand intervention.

Increasingly, an acceptable bypass into iGen's circle of trust is to leverage influencers that already have access to iGen's touch points. These influencers can be bloggers, individuals active on social media, traditional journalists, community leaders, or even just people with a lot of friends. If a brand can ethically earn favor from influencers, then Brian Solis's *one-to-one-to-many* process of communication is leveraged. iGen may not listen to brands, but iGen will listen to influencers they trust when they talk about brands.

There are risks in leveraging influencers for controlled branded communication. Brands must certainly weigh the risks and be careful to choose trusted influencers that have the right target audience. Risks include a complete concession of the brand to a free agent, who may or may not communicate in the style or manner of the brand. However, this concession is often necessary, for if it is known and/or perceived that the influencer is acting on behalf of a brand, then the message will fall on deaf ears. To be credible, the influencer must behave with his or her own voice, opinions, and style. It isn't like traditional media relations, where brands can count on journalists to remain as objective as possible, even with reviews. Influencers are not bound by journalism traditions, nor do they have an investment in protecting any brand's image. They can say what they want and how they want to say it. The cost is risk. However, the return is direct access to a target audience that will listen to the influencer. It provides access a brand does not typically have, and, if done consistently, brands can then earn direct access themselves.

Another consideration when using influencers is that they themselves have a brand of their own to protect. It will do them no favors to come off as a "shill" for a brand, because the fickle community they serve will abandon them the moment they sniff a sellout. The valued trust an influencer earned can easily be lost if they are pushed into using a voice that is not authentic. Further, iGen does not like to be duped. While bloggers in particular and online publishers in general are required by the federal government to disclose payment or product donation information, this can easily be skirted. However, one should not do this. Even if the federal government doesn't know, iGen will find out, and if it is perceived that the influencer was "bought" and wasn't transparent about it, a brand could find itself in a full-on public relations crisis.

While true influencers can be highly valuable in accessing the iGen audience, there are many that do not carry the influence they promote, or if they do, are not influencing the right audience. Brands must take caution when choosing which brand advocates to approach. Does this influencer have a sizable network, offline and/or online? Do they reach the audience that the brand is trying to reach? Do they have a unique voice that their audience consistently and actively responds to? Is there healthy engagement? Does their personal brand align with the brand you are trying to promote? All of these considerations should be thoroughly explored before approaching potential brand advocates. While brands may not be able to control a message through influencers, they can certainly control the influencers with whom they choose to communicate.

In short, partnering with influencers for brand advocacy is an important way to reach iGen, but it must be navigated with care.

Mommy Blogger Revolution

Like most social media trends, mommy blogging took the marketing world by storm, beginning in 2009, culminating in 2011, and continuing its momentum through today. The spike seemed to happen in late 2009, when mommy blogging jumped 50 percent, according to Cision US,[49] and by 2010, mommy bloggers were reaching forty-two million women, 43 percent of whom followed blogs for product recommendations. The trend took storm, and by 2011, major media outlets began plugging into the trend, including the likes of NBC's *Today Show*. Marketers called 2009 the "Year of the Mommy Blogger." They did the same in 2010 and again in 2011.

While this seems to have continued, the buzz around mommy bloggers has softened a little. Brands are starting to understand the impacts and risks associated with leveraging influencers and are more discerning and focused on ROI. Bloggers are significantly more prevalent, and so the search for quality brand advocates is harder than it was.[50] Now that the hype has subsided, it behooves us to examine the mommy blogger movement carefully, because fundamentally, it is a precursor to the core of iGen marketing: finding influential voices to speak about brands to a targeted and otherwise inaccessible audience.

Moms were the first, perhaps because women tend to be strong and active consumers. The female demographic also tends to rely upon trusted word of mouth before making purchases, a hallmark of iGen's behavior. It seems almost natural that women would take the lead on this innovative form of consumer communication. Those who were successful were ethical, transparent, and engaging. They had voices that were, if not humorous, experiential. Other moms trusted these voices because they were peers: women speaking to women.

By 2010 there was a rapid upward trend of daddy bloggers who, in their own distinct voice, achieved much of the same ground as their prolific counterparts. Now, the communication channel is so established, the industry warrants annual conferences, blogger-market relationship management firms, and streamlined processes for brands and bloggers to interact and produce content. By the time iGen enters the arena, mommy/daddy blogging will be such a highly developed institution, it will likely not have the consumer-impacting weight it once did. That said, it is still the model with which iGen best interacts.

What did bloggers and marketers learn from the mommy blogger craze?

- **Ethics:** it took the FTC to crack down on the blogging machine in order for the industry to respond with strict codes of ethical conduct, including transparency and consumer disclosure.

- **Influence:** it wasn't the size of the blogger's network that had the greatest impact; rather it was the relevance of the blogger's audience. Truly effective influencer marketing required a complete understanding of the target audience before approaching the right blogger to fit that audience.

- **Analysis:** blogger-marketer relationships were best managed with clear and achievable objectives and analysis on the impact toward those objectives. Just like any marketing program, influencers must be tracked in order to determine whether or not the effort was worthwhile.

Mommy blogging will continue to be a powerhouse for brands, and our learnings from the revolution will apply to many strategies and tactics in the future. However, it should be recognized that iGen will only listen to iGen, and so they will not be listening to, nor will they be following in the footsteps of, their moms. Mommy blogging will age with the influential moms and will be replaced by a new, still-unforeseen medium for leveraging influencers that can speak to iGen. Whatever the form of that trend, it will follow the same model: consumers listen to other consumers.

The Real World Still Reigns

These days, when one thinks of "word-of-mouth marketing," one most likely thinks of social media. Amazon, Yelp, TripAdvisor (among others), have taken hold of the research phase of the online marketing funnel. Decisions are made in great part by what other consumers have to say about the purchase online. Certainly this extends to Facebook, Twitter, Pinterest, and Google+, where consumers habitually share their consumer experiences with their peers.

But online word of mouth is a very small fraction of the total word of mouth network. As a matter of fact, word of mouth firm, the Keller Fay Group, reports that 90 percent of word of mouth happens offline.[51] According to a Forrester study, $170 billion of retail sales in the US was a result of online sales, while offline sales accounted for 2.3 trillion. These staggering statistics fly in the face of the social media hype we have been accustomed to hearing since 2008.

In the marketing world there was ultimately a backlash against social media as flocks of "gurus" preached that its ability to engage direct with the consumer was the Holy Grail of communications. What they failed to report was that social media engagement and interaction takes consistency and time. It takes time to cultivate a network and it takes time to communicate with a network. It takes so much time, in fact, that many firms hired community managers specifically to manage social media properties. Agencies had to price social media monitoring engagement at a premium to account for the amount of agency hours spent on one client.

Programs had to sit and simmer for months before reaching their maximum capacities.

Also, it was soon realized that social media doesn't deliver an easy-to-measure ROI. Firms tried various ways to attempt to monetize the value of social media, including ad equivalency measurements, used reluctantly by public relations professionals to measure the value of PR. Impressions/size of network alone didn't seem to justify the time spent, and it was difficult to quantify the value of influencers in social media. Sure, top Tweeters may only have impressions of forty thousand, but the value of those impressions is much higher than an online ad. Yet how is that quantified?

Those who embraced social media as a form of reactive consumer engagement discovered its value in customer service. In that context, it isn't a marketing proposition at all but is rather a way of delivering real-time direct access to brand consumers looking for information or problem resolution.

Arguably, the social media movement matured in 2012. Those of us who utilize social media in the professional world understand something that the hype didn't: social media isn't the next be-all-end-all wave of communication. It is a tactic; an arrow in a brand's quiver. Social media in and of itself is a very small fraction of digital communication, which in turn is also a very small fraction of offline communication. Further, social media isn't built for converting prospects into customers, and so it can never truly be paired with ROI metrics. Social media is a cost of doing business, not much different than a website, cell phone, or customer service department. Consumers expect direct access to brands through social media and those who can't get it move on to competitors who can deliver it.

When put in that context then, social media by itself is really a communication channel. Within that channel, marketing programs can be implemented that are tied to sales conversions, ROI, and other profit-making measures. Additionally, branding programs can take place in that channel that can win hearts and minds, communicate brand messages, and provide media impressions. However, it is important to note that the channel by itself is just that: a channel. It isn't a strategy and it isn't a magic bullet designed to reach modern audiences. On the contrary, the modern audience will by and large use these channels for communication when they need something, not to be *sold* to.

That is why social media, like all other channels, must house strategies and tactics designed to reach iGen. Just as it is with traditional media, unless the brand has paid the price of admission, iGen won't listen to brands on Facebook or Twitter either. Social media should be used as part of a holistic approach to reach iGen, because while we know iGen talks to each other online, we also know that 90 percent of the time, they talk to each other *offline*.

Brand Journalism

It has always been critical for brands to have independent advocates. Historically, public relations rested upon the influence of the media to advocate for brands through editorial coverage, product reviews, or opinion pieces. The value of these endorsements trumped traditional advertising because consumers are more inclined to listen to a trusted source than to pay attention to controlled messaging through an ad.

We have witnessed a massive disruption in media consumption over the past five years, however, and consumer attention is now divided between traditional media and influential consumers. This trend has resulted in two situations: firstly, public relations professionals allocate just as many resources to going directly to consumers as they allocate toward traditional media, and secondly, consumers give as much value to other consumers as they do to traditional media.

This trend has been on the upward swing on sites like Amazon and Yelp for quite some time. However, the disruption changed the upward trend into the mainstream status quo. Now with iGen on the horizon, even more stock will be put into peers and consumers than over traditional media. Nielsen reported that consumers trust "real friends" and "virtual strangers" more than newspapers, TV, magazines, or ads.[52] Given other iGen trends, it wouldn't be surprising if that trend increases. While there is a case for public relations to keep a strong focus on consumer influencers, it is not the only trend to keep in mind.

With the decline of traditional media, particularly in print newspapers and magazines, there was an increase in highly skilled, prolific, and unemployed journalists. This new breed of freelance journalists, called "accidental" freelancers, joined the legions of Americans who started their own business during the Great Recession. It is important to note that these accidental freelancers are no less prolific then before, except now they have to market themselves. Just like PR and ad agencies, they have to find clients and get paid by the hour to produce content. The difference, however, is that freelance journalists are still journalists, which already gives them a leg up on consumer trust. A message coming from an ad holds no weight compared to a message coming from a legitimate journalist. What is interesting about the freelance trend is that public relations now has a greater opportunity to "purchase" editorial coverage instead of soliciting it through pitching.

Enter brand journalism. On the surface, the idea of purchasing editorial from a journalist seems, at best, disingenuous and at worst, unethical. However, looking at examples of successful implementation, this can be accomplished successfully, ethically, and effectively simply by being transparent.

Journalists need not necessarily conduct brand journalism. Specifically, brand journalism creates content by a brand as part of its industry's conversation. It isn't content about a brand and/or product. For instance, a brand journalism piece by Ford could be about how drivers can maintain their vehicles and need not even mention Ford. But since it is created by Ford, they are entering the conversation and developing content that is relevant to consumers and that would, in the case of iGen, become a necessary ingredient to their search.

Brand journalism is not the same as an advertorial that

is purchased as an ad and editorialized but is still about a brand and/or product. Brand journalism is the creation of content by a brand that demonstrates expertise about topics relevant to their field, not promotional material designed to convert into a sale. It is industry thought leadership and provides a channel into which brands can insert themselves.

Journalists do make very good brand journalists. With over 150,000 journalists leaving the print media market in the past ten years, it is a natural transition for them. Journalists are hard-wired to remain objective about their editorial work and so will often still operate with the same sort of mindset they had in the past. Additionally, journalists are already thought leaders in the fields they write about, and simply changing the source of their paycheck from a media outlet to a non-media company has very little impact on the type of material they produce. Journalists are prolific. Unlike many copywriters, CEOs, or marketers, journalists are accustomed to producing original and objective content consistently and under deadlines. So it is no wonder that as media companies fail, journalists move into the brand journalist arena.

Critics of brand journalism view this as a form of consumer trickery, whereby journalists go incognito, take a bribe from a corporation, and produce glowing reviews about a product. While it is likely that there are unethical people in the industry, effective brand journalism is honest, transparent, and offers non-promotional content that demonstrates thought leadership and integrates a brand into relevant conversations as an expert.

As demand for traditional media wanes and the War of Relevance escalates, consumers will be less inclined to care about who is paying the personalities from where they get their content, and more about the personalities themselves and the content they create. Therefore, brands are in a perfect position to curate these influencers under a branded banner and let them do what they do best: create engaging and meaningful content to an audience that listens to them.

Curating content using influential journalists goes back

to a strategy paramount to reaching iGen. The new generation will not listen to brands, but they will listen to experts regardless of whether or not they are affiliated with a brand. The trend is already here: Robert Scoble is incredibly influential and highly regarded, yet he is not a journalist nor is he in anyway objective. In fact, he works for a company that sells websites. Pete Cashmore of Mashable is, at his core, a blogger, not a journalist. Even Pulitzer Prize–awarded Huffington Post is much more of a blogging platform and news portal than it is a news outlet. Cisco, IBM, and many other brands are already employing influential journalists to create content; not content *about* them, but content *around* them.

Earning Influencers

Brand journalism is not the only way leveraging influencers that iGen will pay attention to. Age-old media-relations tactics are very effective for leveraging influencers of Brian Solis's *one-to-one-to-many* type. These influencers may be citizen journalists, bloggers, hobbyists, or simply enthusiasts of a particular topic that have a large following. Influencers may have very little influence online but tremendous influence offline, such as educators, musicians, or book groups.

Whatever the influencer a brand pursues, he or she should be qualified. Qualifications need not include whether the person is a journalist or even a good writer. The influencer needs to have a dedicated offline and/or online audience that fits a brand's target audience. Secondly, an influencer's voice must be in alignment with a brand's voice. Should those two qualifications be met, then a pitch can proceed using the same media relations tactics that have always achieved successful stories.

In any event, it is paramount that both the brand and the influencer's arrangement (whether it be paid or product supplied, etc.) are completely transparent to the consumer. Not only is it unethical to secretly "buy" someone's influence, it also violates FTC laws and could get both parties fined. Besides, iGen can smell marketing like a bloodhound, and if they feel duped or slighted, *they* become the influencer and the song won't be a pretty one.

The beauty of iGen's world is that they listen to influencers they trust, and each of the influencer's audiences are also influencers in their own right and, in turn, have an audience that trusts them. It is an innately viral communication space that, when fully engaged, can catapult a brand's message to more people in a more meaningful way than advertising or traditional media endorsements. iGen wants to hear a brand's message; they just don't want to hear it from a brand. Perhaps generations down the road, they will once again have trust in brands, but until then, there is a price of admission. Honesty, transparency, and the freedom to let others say what they feel about your brand is not a very high cost, given what they can offer in return.

Who

Cisco

What Was Going On

By 2011, social media was firmly established in the arsenal of most major companies. Cisco's John Earnhardt, however, wanted to take things to another level. It wasn't enough simply to get editorial coverage of Cisco products and services; he strove to become a thought leader in all topics that Cisco cared about.

What They Did

Cisco created "The Network" and positioned itself as a curator of news and content about all the topics Cisco has an interest in. The company assembled a cast of reporters from prestigious news outlets including the *Wall Street Journal, AP*, and *Bloomberg Businessweek*, and set them to write for Cisco. The result was an information source that was too interesting and relevant for consumers to pass up, and so, seemingly overnight, The Network became its own news outlet, producing and curating relevant content for an audience.

Why It Worked

Cisco identified the very landscape this chapter addresses. Instead of competing with consumer voices, Cisco created content that consumers would look up and/or need during their decision-making process. If Cisco becomes one of the "dots" consumers use to connect with, then the company will already be in the circle of trust when consumers make technology decisions at the point of purchase.

Who

Mommy Bloggers

What Was Going On

With the explosion of mommy bloggers and blogging in general since 2007, marketers jumped onboard to provide free product/payment for public endorsements, essentially misleading readers and propelling unethical media practices. As a result, the FTC updated requirements for testimonials in advertising for the first time since 1980 and required bloggers to disclose material connections with the seller of the product or service.

Why it Didn't Work

Consumers don't like to be tricked, and digital natives can smell marketing from far, far away. Had marketers required transparency from the start, like General Mills and Ford, the FTC would likely not have had to step in. Since 2009, the new FTC guidelines have done little to curb blogger/marketer interactions, and so it just proves that being transparent and ethical does not cost potential digital audiences.

The Net Net

iGen will listen and respond to influencers that they trust, and, as long as all interactions are transparent and ethical, they won't care who is paying the influencer.

Chapter Five

"The People's Capitalism" - The Madison Avenue Swan Song

Why has *American Idol* persisted as one of the top-five-ranked television shows in the United States since 2003?[53] It is certainly not the contestants, who vary from year to year in quality and personality. Nor is it the judges, since after two of the original judges departed in 2009, ratings and viewership stayed exactly the same. The format isn't reason enough, since there are many relatively unsuccessful copycats, such as *The Voice* and *The X-Factor*, and the variety show format itself is an age-old concept.

In 2012, twenty-one million viewers watched the season finale of *American Idol*. The show placed second in overall viewing among the lucrative 18–49 age group. While that was a drop from prior years, *AI* was still in the top five, and the opening show ranked #2. The show has produced five Billboard Music Award winners, four Grammy Award winners, and an Academy Award winner. It rakes in more than $800 million in advertising annually. What made *American Idol* so special that its rivals called it "The Death Star" and "the most impactful show in the history of television"?[54]

Given what we discussed in this book thus far, I would argue that *American Idol* is a national phenomenon simply because the audience determines the winner. Utilizing a yet-untapped process, show creators Simon Fuller and Simon Cowell took Nigel Lythgoe's "*Pop Idol*" model from the UK whereby the television audience voted for the winners via telephone. Although a seemingly simple idea, the mechanism did precisely what Gen Y and iGen have come to expect from their environment: it put them at the driver's wheel.

Arguably, for the first time in modern music history, it is the fans of music who determine which artists should become famous, not the record companies. The model relinquished a tremendous amount of control from the likes of people like Simon Cowell, who agreed to produce the winner based upon popular vote, not upon his professional decision.

American Idol was on the forefront of a much larger trend that began with the maturing of Gen Y. The core Gen Y audience grew up with the show and has now become the nation's most lucrative consumers. By plugging into that pre-social media trend about reverting brand control back to the consumer, *American Idol* managed to win over a marketplace that, until that point, no one knew existed. It may be accurate to say the producers didn't know either, and they were simply responding to a successful model they saw elsewhere.

As *American Idol* matured, so did social technology. After the huge consumer disruption, the show persisted, but not as an innovator, as a mainstream success. Many believe that season 5 in 2006 was the series' peak, featuring Taylor Hicks, Katharine McPhee, and others, and that was, interestingly enough, just as the massive media disruption was beginning. By 2012, *American Idol* was a household name, but it was in decline and will likely continue to be so. But it will forever remain as one of the hallmark institutions of Gen Y and, should it persist long enough, will also be an institution of iGen.

We would do well to look at this model more closely and discover how our brands can succeed in this new environment.

Now that the audience chooses their artists, they will choose their books, their entertainment, and their widgets. This new normal transcends the environment and permeates all brands and products globally, and as we will discover in a later chapter, it even transcends economics, including society and politics. If a variety show on television can thrive in this environment, so can any brand. We need only look at what they did right.

Choose Your Own Adventure

It wasn't that long ago that the record companies produced megastars on a quarterly basis. The so-called "golden age" of rock and roll during the 1950s and 1960s resulted in a monolithic music industry with incredibly deep budgets and tremendous control over pop culture. Few entertainment industries measured up to the music industry at its peak: publishing, television, and film being notable exceptions. At its zenith in 2000, the music industry shipped over one billion "units" (CDs/cassettes/LPs/etc).[55] By 2010, units shipped crested just over three hundred million, less than the number of units shipped in 1973. Concurrent with this industry-wide cataclysmic decline of product sales, singles went from less than one hundred million to over a billion in sales since 2000. Nearly the entire margin was a result of digital downloads. U.S. music revenues reached a low of $9.2 billion, dropping $38 billion since 1999.[56]

The first major reason for the disruption was the release of Napster in 1999, which allowed listeners to trade music for free. By 2003, Apple's iTunes introduced an *à la carte* approach to music purchasing that, coupled with lawsuits and the restructuring of Napster, brought consumers back to a paying model. But with the popularity of the iPod and eventually the iPhone, music consumers became accustomed to picking the single they wanted and not purchasing the full albums that once fed the profitable revenues of record companies. Now that 90 percent of consumers still don't pay for music, while the same margin of those who do pay buy only a song at a time, record companies are left with licensing deals, which, at a measly $84 million a year, did not amount to enough to feed the beast. The "Big 5" record companies of the music industry's heyday was reduced to the "Big 3" by 2011, after the acquisition of EMI by Universal and BMG by Sony.

The music industry has been forever transformed. The days of the big record company are over. Even big-box stores couldn't adapt to the disruption, as seen in the closing of Tower Records and the demise of the neighborhood record store. Consumers are now downloading songs instead of buying albums, and those who do buy albums are ordering them for cents on the dollar at Amazon.com. They are not going anywhere near a retail location unless it is Best Buy or Walmart, where they buy *en masse*, at incredibly steep discounts.

This is a sad narrative for record companies, who for so many decades had their hands on the controls of popular culture. It was the record companies that picked and chose music superstores, funded multi-city stadium tours, fed a marketing machine to propel CDs, cassettes, and LPs out of music stores, produced the videos that MTV put into mainstream consciousness, and ultimately determined, for the consumer, who would be big and who wouldn't.

Consumers now don't go to retail locations and see marketing material and cardboard dumps piled high with the latest releases. MTV is now cluttered with reality TV, leaving out the once influential pop-culture music video machine. DJs are largely automated, and free radio's influence over the consumer has fallen victim to the same fate as other controlled media. What little marketing budgets record companies have are put into advertisements that, like most other ads, are failing due to the dramatic increase of ad-avoidance rates. Like most other legacy industries, the music industry is working to adapt in a world that is now incompatible with its business model.

The music industry is a case in point of how consumers have inverted the communication experience. Before the disruption, we liked Bruce Springsteen because we were told to. After the disruption, we find Bruce Springsteen and tell record companies to promote him. Arguably, because of Napster and Apple's disruption with iTunes, the music industry fell to the consumer-driven marketplace sooner than other industries. In the past five years, however, we have seen identical trends in video rentals (rise of Netflix and fall of Blockbuster), books (rise of Kindle and fall of Borders/ Barnes & Noble), and we are starting to see the trends in television and movies (rise of streaming, fall of live television and movie theaters).

All of these trends are centered on a new normal: the audience, not companies, determines what they like. That point is made very clear when one compares Justin Bieber with Britney Spears.

Britney vs. Justin

Britney Spears and Justin Bieber are both highly successful pop stars. By the age of twenty, both Spears and Bieber topped the Billboard Hot 100, had albums that sold over twenty million copies, and performed at the MTV Video Music Awards. Both artists were, at different times, ranked by *Forbes* as the most powerful celebrity in the world. They both reached global stardom within five years of hitting the music scene.

There is a major difference with their success stories, however. A record company chose Britney, while Justin was chosen by fans.

Britney was originally a cast member on *The Mickey Mouse Club* and, from a very early age, was groomed by music industry professionals for the business. Jive Records, which was specifically looking for another Madonna, Debbie Gibson or Tiffany, picked up Britney. Once signed up for her first album, she was sent on a shopping mall promotional tour coinciding with the album release that topped Billboard

200 and catapulted her to stardom.

Justin was four years old when Britney put out her first album. His discovery came not from record companies but from audiences on YouTube. In 2007, three years after Britney's peak, Justin was uploading his performances online and gaining tremendous viral traction. It took Usher and Justin Timberlake to find Bieber on YouTube before record companies took notice. By the time Usher found Bieber, his videos had over four hundred thousand views. By 2012, he had four hundred million views on YouTube and broke a YouTube record when he released a single that reached eight million views within twenty-four hours. By mid-2012, Justin had over twenty million followers on Twitter, resulting in a comment from Twitter officials that stated, "Racks of servers are dedicated to Bieber."

Britney is no stranger to social media either, having more than 60 million views on YouTube and seventeen million followers on Twitter. However, it was Justin who paved the way. His sharp and record-breaking climb through social media was the impetus for other celebrities, including Spears.

Justin's popularity fits the mold of *American Idol*'s popularity and is, in many ways, indicative of the future of entertainment. The audience *chose* Justin Bieber, and his rise to fame did not require the wholesale marketing push that Britney Spears did.

Now, this doesn't mean that celebrities will only be found on social media, but it does represent a change in consumer consciousness. Consumers will like what they like, whether or not brands are marketing to them. For record companies, this may mean giving contracts to artists who already have a following, or crowdsourcing the next star. It also means that record companies will have a very difficult time creating their own sensations from scratch.

The End of Propaganda

Nearly 50 percent of Americans skip TV and radio ads or avoid websites with intrusive pop-up advertising, and of those who watch ads, only 50 percent care and/or understand the ad message delivered.[57] What's more, 72 percent of Americans find advertising "annoying." Ads aside, fewer Americans are paying attention to the news.[58] The top-down method of communicating to the audience is no longer effective. In other words, controlled messaging designed to control perceptions is increasingly ignored or not impactful.

When we look at the successes of Justin Bieber and *American Idol* and compare them to the traditional *modus operandi* of the music industry, the conclusion is clear. Just like with other scenarios discussed in this book, the reigns of control must be handed over to music fans for the music industry to thrive.

The Generation Gap(s)

As we explore these trends in the context of iGen, we can see the stark generational differences. Baby Boomers were about consuming: purchasing the American Dream and living in an environment for which they paid. iGen is about developing their own version of the American Dream and creating new environments catered specifically to them.

Generation X was about "us versus the man," where ideals were built upon individuality and creativity, naturally positioning themselves against the institutions their parents financed. iGen is about "the man versus us," where the tables have turned and the institutions shunned by the parents of iGen are now catering personally to their demands.

Gen Y was the "me" generation, the first digital natives who prized personal achievements without personal failures and created a world void of competition. iGen is the "us" generation, who escalate the Gen Y platform to include not only individuals, but also all individuals who, together, can mold and shape the environment they want.

These are swooping generalizations of consumer behavior, certainly not true of all individuals or even groups of individuals. However, as marketers, we need to take a look at these trends, understand how they differ from one another, and analyze the resulting environment these trends will lead to.

In many ways, it is the perfect economy: the "people's capitalism," where consumers determine the outcomes based upon what is best for each individual consumer and the market as a whole. Companies now need to elevate competition to not only include price and market share, but also to compete for the favor of their consumers, which will force their hand into more innovation, higher quality, and a fine understanding of their target audiences. It is the work marketers should have been doing all along, but is now crucial to their success.

Old-hat tactics like advertising, media relations and consumer engagement, brand partnerships, and crowdsourcing will replace big-box marketing. It is a brave new world, and if Blockbuster, Tower Records, and Borders have taught us one thing, it is that we should be focusing on propelling the Justin Biebers of the world.

But What of the Experts?

If it is true that the consumers are now choosing their stars, art, culture, music, and literature, then it is also true that popular culture is determining the quality of products, not the experts. In legacy industries, there were entire career fields devoted to telling audiences what was good and bad: product reviewers, film/music/book critics, and consumer journalists. To get a positive book review in the *New York Times* meant a sure shot at the *New York Times* Best Sellers List; to receive a favorable album review in *Rolling Stone* meant you would top the radio charts; to get a nod from *Forbes* would mean your business-to-business services would be noticed.

But if *American Idol* and Justin Bieber are any indicator

of tomorrow's economy, the expert will only be heard if he or she is a trusted source for iGen, and iGen generally chooses only their own. Does this mean readers only read book and music reviews on Amazon and film reviews on Rotten Tomatoes? If that is the case, is there a place for the authority in the industry to inform consumers what is good and bad?

The job of "critic" was once a specialized one that required tremendous knowledge and measurable industry experience. They could tell you a particular album was terrible because they had spent their professional life learning enough about music to know what was good and what was bad. The restaurant critic, the film critic, the book reviewer, the product reviewer—they were all in the business of knowing their field and informing the public so they could make informed decisions.

If everyone is a critic and iGen only listens to each other, what role does the professional critic have? Isn't there be something to be said for the value of a professional critic—a journalist, steeped in his or her field, who can knowledgeably inform audiences about art and culture, or are reviews now relegated to the caprices of uninformed peers who have baseless opinions swaying audiences on a whim?

For iGen, the traditional critic is not influential, but when we consider that traditional media is still the source for news and information, even in social media, then the role of the critic becomes clear. The critic is the "baseline" from which peers and consumers can measure their own opinions. Therefore, the professional critic must be inserted into one of the "dots" that iGen uses to process information. A critic can still influence iGen if they curate peer reviews along with their own.

Rotten Tomatoes is a perfect implementation of the new normal in consumer-driven reviews. The site features moviegoer reviews right alongside professional reviews, then compares and contrasts them, linking them all up in a social environment. Since audiences are going to Rotten Tomatoes anyway to see what their peers thought of a movie, the professional reviews would automatically serve as a baseline. The moviegoer can compare reviews and see who seems more off base: the professional or the average moviegoer. What they choose to go see is subsequent to the point that they used traditional media as *one of the dots* that connected their decision.

iGen may not go to the *New York Times* to read a movie review, but they will go to a website of audience reviews and see a *New York Times* review. Amazon's collection of reviews accomplishes the same with books and music.

Therefore, when marketing products to iGen, traditional media is still absolutely necessary. Otherwise there would be no baseline with which to compare nonprofessional opinions. However, for traditional media reviews to be seen, they must be implemented along with nonprofessional reviews in a virtual or physical location that iGen uses to find information about your product.

Successful curation is ultimately the way a product, person, band, widget, etc. can be transformed into Justin Bieber, even if it started as Britney Spears.

Who

Pepsi

What Was Going On

In 2010, Pepsi was looking for new ways to reach audiences and decided to allocate its Super Bowl budget to a new social media program.

What They Did

Pepsi created *Pepsi Refresh* with a $20 million budget, a philanthropic program housed in an interactive social media platform that called for individuals and organizations to raise money for causes. The community voted for the causes that they believed should get funding. By the end of 2010, there were sixty-one million votes cast and $14.6 million granted to fund 352 causes.

Why It Worked

The structure of Pepsi Refresh accomplished two things that resonated with the post-disruption audience: it focused on philanthropy (a factor important to iGen, as will be discussed in a future chapter), and it required that the audience choose what causes would get grant money. Not only was this approach elegantly interactive and social, but it also built willing brand advocates who would use their own networks to publicize their cause. Because they were using their own networks, they broke through the audience's barrier of trust and accessed their infinite touch points.

Who

Advertisers in the Super Bowl XLVI

What Was Going On

Historically, the Super Bowl is the most coveted television ad spot in the country, and in 2010, ads were costing upward of $3 million per thirty-second spot. A whopping 62 percent of marketers had a negative ROI from that Super Bowl, and those with a positive ROI (upward of 11 percent) were snack food commercials or controversial Super Bowl ads. 8.4 percent of Super Bowl audiences said the commercials influenced them to buy products, so even at that number, only fourteen million would have been reached by a Super Bowl ad.

What They Did

Super Bowl ads must rely upon creativity and humor to reach audiences, and, due to that expectation, these ads had a much lower ad-avoidance rate. However, the cost is brand retention. Viewers may watch the ads, but they may not remember what the ad was for, and even then, that may not convert into a sale. It is still a controlled media channel that is becoming increasingly ineffective with ad-avoiding audiences. In the years after 2010, brands made ads far more interactive, which resulted in increased ROI.

The Net Net

iGen chooses their rock stars now, so market the rock stars they choose, not the ones you choose.

Chapter Six

"Beatles or Elvis?" - The Lifestyle Badge

According to a deleted scene from Quentin Tarantino's *Pulp Fiction* (1994), there are Elvis fans and Beatles fans, and, while both can enjoy Elvis and the Beatles, they will always love one over the other. Like many other lines in the movie, this notion became an adage, and studies were even done to confirm its accuracy. Interestingly, it seems pop culture often has personality divisions such as this: Clint Eastwood vs. John Wayne, Michael Jackson vs. Prince, Schwarzenegger vs. Stallone, Bieber vs. Spears, etc.

Ultimately, these "personality tests" are the result of a fundamental need for people to identify themselves with a symbol. Civilization has been doing this for years: family crests, banners, sigils, and tartans . . . the list goes on. Just because we don't need flags to identify each other on the battlefield anymore doesn't mean we have stopped representing ourselves with symbols. These days we are less formal about it: avatars, profile images, matching T-shirts, on family vacations, etc.

Facebook added a new layer to this human phenomenon. With the invention of the "like" button, billions of people all over the world began publicly declaring what they liked and, by omission, what they don't like. With each "like," people can show all of their friends something about themselves. On one hand, it is the virtual equivalent of "Hey, I like Led Zeppelin too!" On the other hand, it is much more significant.

Whether or not it was intentional, the Facebook Timeline has become a very thorough and interactive vehicle for public self-expression; Facebook and the Facebook culture allows for individuals to *brand* themselves.

This is significant because at no time since the cola wars has there been such a tremendous opportunity for brands of all kinds to become lifestyle badges for consumers. For all of the challenges of accessing iGen, the plentiful reward of selfless brand advocacy is unprecedented. Brands that align with iGen's personal brand are shamelessly displayed as a part of their personal identity. While this is most evident on Facebook Timelines where users check-in places, "like" brands, and share purchases, the trend is permeating throughout consumer behavior.

Social media may be the medium for this new enhanced brand-advocacy trend, but it doesn't stop there. Rather, social media is a conduit that escalates the brand conversation into other online and offline channels. The net result is that consumers create an online thumbprint that publicly identifies themselves, their unique interests, passions, and behaviors.

All that is left for the marketer is to undergo consumer archeology and uncover what values drive their target audience, and how the brands can genuinely align themselves with those values, in order to connect with the new empowered level of brand advocacy. Being liked on Facebook is the first step, but there is an extended courting process that, when delivered, plugs into the one-to-one-to-many network of brand influencers and accesses iGen's infinite touch points.

The Facebook Self

Facebook is like a college dorm room. I don't mean that it is full of immature drunken banter and photographs demonstrating reckless discretion; rather that the Facebook walls hold "posters" that publicly reveal a person's identity. When you show up to college and your roommate has posters of the Oakland Raiders and you are about to put up posters of the 49ers, then you already know basically what to expect from one another. Similarly, Batman posters separate those who put up Spiderman posters, etc. The point is this: students publicly brand themselves by choosing posters that best symbolically describe who they are.

The Facebook Timeline does the same thing, except that the dimensions of the dorm room walls are infinite, and the dormitory has billions in residence. Since Facebook's popularity exploded roughly by 2008–2009, there have been many to quickly criticize the tendency for users to "over-share."

As one *Time* columnist put it after a Facebook meme that encouraged users to write "25 Things about Me": "Most people aren't funny, they aren't insightful, and they share WAY too much."[59] Then there are those Facebook users who learned the hard way that thoughts that were normally kept between friends were not the same as thoughts that are shared with Facebook friends. There are quite a few accounts of people who disparaged their bosses at work, went surfing after calling in sick, or complained about customers, only to find themselves without a job.

This rash of over-sharing was in great part a result of Facebook's confusing privacy settings. Many users didn't realize just how "visible" their posts, photo uploads, and photo tags were. It would be fair to say that most Facebook users have wised up by now and are much more careful about what they share and with whom. Facebook has also gone to great lengths to make their privacy settings more user-friendly and accessible, much to their chagrin. The company was founded on the concept of social interaction and therefore was reluctant to put up too many privacy barriers.

Still, privacy settings aside, there is a tremendous urge to share one's thoughts on Facebook as if in a coffee shop, restaurant, or bar, surrounded by friends. Certainly the social network is entirely based on the concept of "friends." Coming into the environment with that notion automatically puts users in a "friendlier/chattier" disposition. They are far more willing to be honest and forthright about their thoughts and opinions and are encouraged to continue this behavior, especially when comments or likes begin appearing on their posts.

Facebook psychologically "games" (or drives) users into interacting with one another. A psychology study found that Facebook causes "high positive valence and high arousal" when compared to both relaxed states and stress states. In other words, Facebook scientifically makes us feel good.[60]

According to the study, there are two reasons for this: the first is that people want to feel connected. The social network is designed for us to interact with one another, and so we connect with others far more easily and quicker than with other methods, feeding us needed human interaction but requiring very little effort. Secondly, Facebook is very effective in tapping into our need for self-presentation; that is, creating an "ideal" of one's self, rather than the accurate version of themselves. In other words, Facebook allows people to brand themselves.

Facebook works because of the ease by which people can interact with one another and the ability to create an idealized personal identity. It is the perfect storm of psychological fulfillment. People "over-share" on Facebook because of a primal need to be accepted, to fit in, and to run with the pack. They interact with brands, pages, locations, and other people as a strategic way to create a perception of who they are: an idealized perception. Facebook allows people to promote their best parts and quickly find packs that would accept those attributes.

Undoubtedly, the successful psychology game Facebook plays is here to stay. iGen is being raised in a world where parents check in with photos wherever they go and people from all over the country like and comment on those photos. When iGen checks into prom, Aunt Susie in Sacramento can tell them how pretty their dresses are. When iGen visits the Statue of Liberty, their friends back home can say, in real time, that they wished they were there.

Whenever iGen goes to a restaurant, reads a book, listens to a song, gets groceries, goes dancing, or gets a haircut, they will take hundreds, if not thousands, of people with them—all along, ideologically, building a public perception of who they are, what they like, and why they belong in their immense social circles.

Truly, this has phenomenal implications for marketers. The task then is to look at the idealized persona a person creates on Facebook and communicate a brand message that plugs perfectly into that specific lifestyle. With iGen, all brands are lifestyle brands. They are choosing how to publicly present themselves to a carefully crafted audience. When they like the Starbucks fan page, they aren't doing it to get news and updates on lattes. They are doing it to say, "I'm a busy person on the go who doesn't settle for low-brow coffee." When they like the Coffee Bean, they are saying, "I enjoy coffee as a connoisseur and take the time to enjoy it." When they like the independent coffee shop downtown they are saying, "I'm out of the mainstream and choose coffee from locals, not corporations."

As a matter of fact, every post, interaction, check-in, or photo is a demographic analysis of a target audience. Hotel check-ins, *Wall Street Journal* post shares, and photos of weekend barbecues all paint a very different picture than nightclub check-ins, *People* magazine post shares, and photos of friends drinking margaritas.

What is significantly different with iGen from any other generation is that *once you are given access*, you can find out absolutely anything about them that you want. To get the pouring over-sharing faucet of iGen, marketers must align their brand with the lifestyle brand of iGen. When that is done, they will check in with you, post about you, like you, and become highly influential brand advocates that give you access to a very attentive and reactive audience.

It begins by putting out the right message. The next step

is to make a connection. To do that, one must understand how Facebook has changed the definition of "friend."

The New Friend

Sometime last year, our office had an in-depth discussion over the definition of "friend" during a staff meeting. A staff member had asserted that she only added real-life friends on Facebook, and a discussion ensued because she had over five hundred friends on Facebook. Did she really have five hundred real-life friends, or did she have five hundred people with whom she had a real-life connection? For her, a member of Gen Y, there was no differentiation. Interestingly, the debate was between colleagues of her age and colleagues of mine (Gen X). The Gen X position was that no one has five hundred real-life friends. As the discussion wrapped, it became clear that Gen Y and Gen X were defining the word "friend" very differently.

Anecdotally, I have found that those within my generation have a close group of friends, perhaps not surpassing ten or twelve people. These are people who will do anything you ask without question, because they know you will do so in return. They are people who attend family gatherings, can be relied upon to help during a move, and have relationships that likely go back many, many years.

Beyond that close group of friends are acquaintances and colleagues. They may be people you work with, or have worked with at some point. They may be in your extended professional network, or may have been dorm roommates, high school classmates, perhaps extended family, mentors, business partners, or investors. It is quite possible that this extended network could reach five hundred or more, though that would be quite the influential person (not uncommon in the PR industry).

Beyond that are individuals with whom you have connections but no relationship, such as vendors; potential vendors; customers; business proprietors whom you meet at events, parties, or trade shows, etc. Certainly this number could reach several hundred as well.

It became clear that our Gen Y colleague viewed anyone she had personally met as a friend. In that case, one's friendship circle could easily reach five hundred. But it begs the question, How much influence does one have with these so-called friends? Is my influence stronger with, say, my college roommate than with the manager of a bagel shop I frequent? One would think not, but astonishingly, because of Facebook, that may very well be the case.

Gen Y-ers will be the first to tell you that one should not rely upon Facebook friends in cases such as emergencies or emotional support. However, when it comes to influence, Gen Y is equally influenced by real-life friends as they are by Facebook friends. Additionally, Facebook fans will interact with all Facebook friends equally, regardless of the proximity of their real-life relationships. This is because Facebook levels the playing field and, as long as someone is putting out content friends are interested in, they will interact, regardless of their real-life connection.

iGen will follow this pattern. Geographical, political, and social barriers are all but removed on Facebook. Proximity of friendships will be far less important than quality of engagement with people online. iGen will have their real-life friends too, but the virtual friends will be weighted as just as important.

When addressing iGen from a marketing point of view, this is significant. Their circle of influence is far larger than any prior generation. They can influence near strangers just as effectively as best friends. They are less discerning about whom they bring into their sphere of influence. Most importantly, they advocate for brands to their sphere of influence, when the brand aligns with their personal brand.

The Virtual Thumbprint

Internet users realized, in some cases too late, that since the advent of social media, their online actions are permanently and publicly tracked. Each interaction nearly anywhere on the web is tracked and linked to other locations on the web, resulting in a highly visible trail that is indexed and tracked by powerful search engines. Simply Googling anyone you know will yield specific real-time results that reveal that person's footprint online and ultimately who that person is.

Comments and ratings on Amazon and eBay, Yelp reviews, Facebook posts, tweets, comments on blogs, links shared on Digg, songs listened to on Spotify, items pinned on Pinterest, news articles read on Huffington Post; they are all aggregated and put into search engine databases for the world to see. This new reality will create major innovations in privacy boundaries and protection, but those that were not careful about privacy settings laid it out for all the world to see.

Now potential employers look applicants up on Facebook and LinkedIn; estranged spouses follow the actions of their exes; investors study the value of leaders in potential investment companies; competitors watch competitors; lawyers look for evidence in cases; and the media scours for insights on politicians, celebrities, and corporate leaders. The world is watching everything anyone does.

This reality, while possibly disturbing to some, is the price we pay for a free Internet. Like any information channel, it is critical that individuals and organizations control the distribution of information so that when people do investigate, they find only things you want them to find. Few realized how much information has been released since the online social media disruption of 2007–2008.

These tracked and aggregated footprints eventually became thumbprints: unique online imprints that specifically identify individuals. Those wise to these thumbprints can carefully craft an online image for themselves and, ultimately, a personal brand. Also, the wise ones will carefully control the distribution of information so that any online activity accurately reflects their personal brand.

As marketers, it is our task to carefully examine these thumbprints and ensure that when communicating to our target audience, we are appealing to their brand. With iGen, communication is more akin to strategic partnership and brand alignment programs than to simple publicity or advertising. We need to convince iGen that we are a perfect brand partner, aligned with their lifestyle and image—that we are a brand they would be proud to wear on their Facebook wall and tell their friends about. We are not trying to convert consumers anymore; we are trying to forge brand partnerships. Understanding that distinction is fundamental for accessing iGen's infinite touch points.

Consumer Archeology

Marketers must thoroughly explore their target audience before attempting to align brands with personal brands. This has always been true, but is paramount with iGen. It is not enough to generalize audiences, put them into large buckets, and sandblast a message, hoping that some of it sticks. Marketers will need to do two things: determine their audience and then conduct thorough market research about their audience before attempting to engage iGen on their own lifestyle turf.

There are, of course, plenty of tools and services to help marketers understand their audiences, but before research takes place, the brand must take careful measure of their target audience. Whom do they want to reach and why? With iGen, it isn't good enough to slap a gender and age-range as a target audience. Brands must identify the lifestyle they want to target, and the rest comes after that. Mountain bikers? Hip hop concertgoers? Theater lovers? Environmentally conscious? Small business conscious? Craft beer drinkers? Premium coffee drinkers? Organic food eaters? With iGen, these lifestyle qualities are far more telling than age, gender, or occupation.

For instance, take natural food grocery brands. Whole Foods and Trader Joes serve two different lifestyle brands. While they often interconnect, they are distinctly different. Both lifestyles prefer natural and organic foods, enjoy high-quality products, and expect high levels of customer service. Yet Whole Foods customers pay more for gourmet items while Trader Joes customers pay less for unique items. It would be easy to categorize both customers into the same natural foods, affluent, 35–45 age group, and that may be accurate, but it isn't telling the whole story. Whole Foods represents a different lifestyle than Trader Joes, just like Starbucks represents a different lifestyle than Coffee Bean. At which store does a thrifty, health-conscious hobbyist chef shop, and at which store does an affluent, high-stressed professional with sophisticated taste shop?

Many of these swooping generalizations of Whole Foods customers and Trader Joes customers are anecdotal and are asserted without research. Starting there, however, marketers need to implement consumer archeology, dissecting the lifestyle that is most attractive to a marketer's brand. Starting with a gut check, marketers can ask for the perfect target audience that shops at Whole Foods (or drives a Prius, or whatever lifestyle brand applies). Then, using anecdotal evidence, the marketer can draw a picture of who that person is in other aspects of his or her life. What car does the customer drive, what kinds of groceries does he or she buy, where does he or she take a vacation, etc.?

Once all of the ideal consumer qualities are outlined and lifestyle brands isolated, the marketer then conducts "consumer archeology" to uncover the specific behavior patterns that define the lifestyle group. This means looking on lifestyle brand social media outlets and observing how they interact and the types of content they share and post, or visiting lifestyle-oriented blogs and reading comments to dive into how the target audience perceives and responds to specific things. In other words, consumer archeology is about figuring out what your ideal consumer's online thumbprint is. Knowing age, gender, and age group is far subsequent to knowing how they present their personal brand online.

Remember, iGen has created an idealized version of themselves online: a personal brand. You have to know their brand if you intend to align your brand with theirs. When the thumbprint has been mapped out and a marketer is certain about all the lifestyle qualities of their target audience, then the real work begins. The marketer creates controlled messages designed specifically to plug into their target audience's personal brand and in so doing, creates a brand partnership that ultimately leads to brand advocacy.

Don't Dream It, Be It

To be successful, it is not enough to create a brand message that fits with a target audience's lifestyle brand. The brand itself must genuinely be a good match for the target audience's lifestyle. Creating a message just to attract the right people will fall flat the moment those people realize the message does not accurately represent the real brand; as an example, BP is having a tough time convincing people they are environmentally responsible.

Brands should not simply attempt to plug into a lifestyle brand for the sake of doing it. There should be a genuine likeness and affinity, just as is true when brand partnerships are formed on the B2B level. It should make sense. Of course mountain bikers would like the Nature Valley granola bar fan page. They wouldn't necessarily like a Snickers fan page no matter how many times Snickers "satisfies" after exercise. Mountain bikers and Nature Valley brands naturally align; Snickers doesn't.

iGen can sniff out market washing. They know if companies are being insincere about the environment, the economy, small business, etc. Remember that they know about your brand long before your messages reach them. Brands can't lie, be insincere, be misleading; nor can they spin or put lipstick on a pig. iGen is smarter than brands. They know marketing when they see it, and while they will be the first to ignore a brand message, they will equally embrace it if the message genuinely fits their lifestyle. They will wear it as a badge of honor so that the entire world can see the ideal person they want to be.

Visual Literacy

Another phenomenon that is fueling iGen's online footprint and brand identity is the increased visual nature of the web. The status update is systematically being replaced by visual updates: photos, images, memes, and videos. The peak of the status update in 2006, when Twitter and Facebook Newsfeed was introduced, was recently overwhelmed by the rise of Instagram, Pinterest, Google+, and, most notably, Flipboard. This visually displayed news app has become the standard of how information is aggregated: visually, not textually. The trend is dramatic: Pinterest acquired 10.4 million users by February 2012. Facebook bought Instagram for $1 billion in 2012. Image and animated gif leader, Tumblr, will eclipse "blog" in Google popularity. Infographics are increasingly a solid method for conveying information and receiving engagement from readers.

Because Internet consumers are behaving and interacting visually, they will increasingly bypass content that is not visual. iGen may not notice non-visual media, at all.

Who

Starbucks

What Was Going On

During a particularly divisive election season in the summer of 2012, Starbucks CEO Howard Schultz, published an open letter about how, on Independence Day, Americans should come together and celebrate America and not be politically divided. He also offered a free cup of coffee to anyone who came into Starbucks that day, asking that customers tweet innovative ideas using the #INDIVISIBLE hashtag.

What They Did

Thousands participated on Twitter and Facebook, sharing the free coffee promotion and the message behind it. It did well to promote the already successful Jobs for USA program.

Why It Worked

Social responsibility aside (a big factor for Starbucks' successful marketing program), the CEO tapped into a specific consumer trend he knew his target audience was experiencing: election fatigue. Further, he sealed the deal by creating a message his audience would proudly stand behind and therefore advocate. Starbucks is aligning their brand with a complex and socially responsible lifestyle brand, a perfect match for their target audience.

Who

Paula Dean

What Was Going On

Paula Deen, host of the Food Network's "Paula's Best Dishes" is known for cooking high-fat, sugar-heavy foods. Early in 2012, she announced on the Today Show that she was diagnosed with type 2 diabetes three years prior. At the same time, she announced a partnership with diabetes drug-maker Novo Nordisk, which had, apparently, contracted with her to serve as a spokesperson.

What They Did

There was a public outcry from the media, other celebrity chefs, and the medical community regarding Deen's and Novo Nordisk's tactics. It was perceived that Dean's promotion of unhealthy foods after having been diagnosed was considered hypocritical. Further, Novo Nordisk's willingness to use a celebrity who advocates unhealthy foods as a spokesperson was equally criticized.

Why It Didn't Work

Novo Nordisk was likely trying to reach a target audience prone to having diabetes. Knowing that Paula Deen served this audience, it was thought a partnership would make sense if she came out with having diabetes. The public perceived this as "washing" and disingenuous; Paula was clearly not changing her lifestyle, and Novo Nordisk was not trying to send a better message to her audience.

The Net Net

All brands are lifestyle brands to iGen, and so they will advocate for a brand if it supports their idealized public persona.

Chapter Seven

"Power to the People, Right On" - The Social Currency

In 2011, *Time* magazine's person of the year was "The Protester," characterized mostly by the Arab Spring, which began in Tunisia and then spread throughout the Middle East, but also by political protests in Spain, China, Greece, and even the U.S. It was remarkable how the activist movement washed over the globe; each movement had a very unique reason. Whatever the cause for the protests, the location, or the people involved, there was one attribute in common: social media was the primary vehicle for communication.

For the first time in history, groups could organize in real time right under the nose of their oppressors and release information to the outside world. In the Middle East, dictators had no way to stop, control, or regulate social media interactions with protesters and revolutionaries; even drastic measures such as shutting down communication channels did little to stop the flood of information that went to the media and communities outside of the region. It was an unprecedented reversal of control from the institutions to the people, and, just like in the business world, the only recourse was for governments to concede control to the masses.

The Arab Spring, the economic crisis in the Eurozone, and U.S. politics all share the dramatic effects of people-controlled media. The larger point here is not necessarily that social media made this possible; it is that there are no longer communication boundaries in the world. The protester movement made distant problems real and identifiable to people in the West. Suddenly, global issues were not too far away to take notice but were rather injected into our media consumption. iGen is growing up in a world where what happens in Egypt, Greece, and North Korea directly affects what is going on in Wisconsin, Rhode Island, and Arizona.

There are many consequences of this, but perhaps the most dramatic consequence of having the world's problems on their shoulders is that iGen and Gen Y expect everyone to contribute to solving these problems. Unlike prior generations, digital natives are acutely interested in solving social issues and making small but consistent movements toward positive change in the world they live in. This could be because they were born with 9/11 at their doorstep, or perhaps because they witnessed the Great Recession, but it also has a great deal to do with the fact that the world is much more visible than it ever has been before. We can see across continents with no inhibitions, barriers, or filters. We see how people truly are, not how the media, governments, or marketers portray people to be.

Being a marketer in this type of environment, then, it is crucial that companies don't think of corporate social responsibility as a budget-line item. It is a paramount obligation for access into iGen's circle of trust. Cause marketing is not a fad, it is a success metric no different than profit margins or stock prices. In most cases, it is not enough simply to market or benefit a cause, it also needs to be ingrained into a brand's identity.

Brands Are People

The 2012 election season in the U.S. was ripe with the notion that corporations are "people," and while I am not interested in entering that particular discussion, it is important to note that iGen *expects* brands to be people. The days of a faceless corporation delivering products based upon marketing-produced demand are over. iGen wants to know they are buying from people, and the reason they want to know that is because they want to make sure the people they are buying from fit their brand identity.

How can iGen proudly wear a brand on their shirt and flaunt their advocacy for the brand if they don't know they are aligned with the brand, and, further, how can they know if they are aligned with the brand if they don't know the people behind the brand? The cult of personality has always resonated with digital natives: Mark Zuckerberg, Steve Jobs, Biz Stone—this is because they know the people behind the organization and can therefore align themselves with them.

One very recent example of this happened in the men's razor market. For decades, Gillette and Schick have been perceived as gouging the market by charging exorbitant prices for razors. The "faceless" razor corporation has the market share and distribution, so men largely have no choice but to pay for their highly marked-up product.

Enter Dollar Shave Club. A single video took the web by storm, yielding over four million views in under a month, featuring the CEO of Dollar Shave Club explaining why his razors are "f***ing great" and that for just a dollar a month, you can have them shipped to your door. It was a thumb in the face of the faceless corporation and showed an arrogant, but hilarious face that can be identified with. Now, while iGen is largely not yet in the razor market, this ad would certainly fulfill all of the qualifications of a perfect iGen product.

Firstly, it assumes the audience is sick of the institution/corporation/status-quo. Secondly, it uses viral humor to demonstrate that this small company is also sick of it. Thirdly, it promises that by sticking it "to the man," you can come out ahead and have a good product. Dollar Shave Club made itself human and demonstrated value. The results were dramatic: the company racked up twelve thousand customers in just two days. If Gen Y is jumping on this, so will iGen. But iGen would likely not have considered Gillette in the first place.

There is no reason why large and established brands can't be humanized. This book has already addressed many examples of successful brands that have done just that: Ford, Old Spice, Starbucks, Pepsi . . . the point is that iGen does not reject brands simply because they are a function of marketing, from a corporation, or created by "the man." On the contrary, they will embrace brands that they can identify with. One quick way to accomplish that is to make a brand human, identifiable.

As Funny or Die's VP of marketing, Patrick Starzan, told *Fast Company*, "Everyone says—kids especially—they don't want to be marketed to or advertised to. That's not true. They don't want to be talked down to."

Social Responsibility

Beyond only humanizing brands, iGen expects a brand to be committed to social responsibility. Edelman's Good Purpose Study showed that 76 percent of consumers believe it is okay for brands to support good causes and make money at the same time, and 53 percent stated that social purpose ranks as the most important factor in selecting a brand, up 26 percent since last year.[61] If one considers that over 50 percent of the world's population consists of digital natives, then that 26 percent jump could be attributed to them. Perhaps most astonishingly, 87 percent believe that business needs to give at least the same weight to society's interest as it does to business interests.

Another study by the AMP Agency said that 83 percent of people would trust a socially active company, 74 percent would pay attention to cause-based marketing, and if price and quality were equal, 89 percent are likely to switch from one brand to another when they are affiliated with a good cause.[62]

A recent global study of iGen parents said that a staggering 71 percent of moms agree that their kids know about what is happening in the world.[63]

These statistics are demonstrating an important trend. Commitment to social issues should be in the fabric of a successful iGen-targeted brand. There is an opportunity for misstepping here, however. For all of those who support cause-conscious brands, just as many reject those that are not sincere in cause marketing. The activity of "cause washing," or using a cause superficially to promote a brand, can have a tremendous negative effect on a brand. iGen is not receptive to either inflating one's concern for a cause or using a cause as a crutch in marketing.

The documentary *Pink Ribbons, Inc.*, released in spring of 2012, dove deeply into cause marketing surrounding breast cancer pink ribbon campaigns. It spotlighted how companies exploit the cause in order to market products and the disproportionate allocation of funds raised going to the medical industry instead of to cure research. Clearly, there is a thin line between genuinely contributing to a cause and superficially supporting a cause. According to Edelman's studies, the former will earn trust, but the latter will break it.

As the "mother of cause marketing," Carol Cone from Edelman said at the release of their study, "Cause marketing is dead . . . purpose has replaced cause marketing and branding."[64] Further along, the panel discussed the difference between real and fake purpose. Ultimately the findings show that brands have to (a) commit to improving society and (b) be transparent and genuine in doing so.

iGen cares that brands care. They can connect with them as people, align with their purpose, and in so doing, become a brand advocate. iGen is not looking to criticize brands, nor are they cynical about brands. On the contrary, brands are receiving unprecedented support and advocacy from digital natives. However, it is more important to iGen that they create positive social change, and they will expect that same sentiment from their brand partners.

Social Entrepreneurship

While not a new trend, social entrepreneurship is taking a grip in the newly disrupted world. Social entrepreneurism, the act of spotting a social problem and then using innovation to solve the problem on a large scale, has taken root in both non-profit and for-profit organizations. Since the rise of cause marketing, social entrepreneurs have found tremendous resources from the private sector, and they have done impactful work in promoting positive changes in society.

The impetus for increased social entrepreneurship was likely attributable to the Great Recession when both governments and corporations were looking for innovations that would solve major society issues in order to bring back prosperity. Environmental crises, political upheaval, and other major global trends have also created a demand for social enterprise, and when paired with communications technology and the removal of global barriers, the landscape is ripe to make large-scale change utilizing business strategies and tactics.

Social entrepreneurs collaborate with communities, organizations, and for-profit groups on creating comprehensive and scalable solutions to large-scale problems. Examples of such collaborations are the Triple Bottom Line methodology used in environmental social entrepreneur circles that require contributions from all stakeholders, regardless if they are residents, business owners, or community leaders.[65] This model of addressing problems is unlike traditional nonprofit approaches because altruism and ideology are trumped by bottom-line sensibility of business; at the same time, it is unlike traditional business approaches because it includes social welfare as an asset in the bottom-line formula.

As this social enterprise trend continues to emerge, the line will be further blurred between for-profits and nonprofits because both groups will be working to achieve the same social good. Additionally, capitalism itself is in a metamorphosis that, according to millionaire Richard Branson, should value social good and not only financial good. Now that global barriers are down, social problems have become business problems that need real comprehensive solutions.

As iGen matures and begins to compare brands based upon how much they can personally contribute to their society, they will see legacy brands that put money into causes, if not superficially, then without commitment, and they will see brands that have integrated social responsibility as a part of their fabric. For iGen, the choice will be simple.

As Branson said, successful companies will understand that the purpose of a brand is ultimately for the social good. Companies that are established in order to resolve a social problem have statistically far more profitability and success than companies that don't. With iGen's sensibilities in mind, brands should be developed so that the brand cannot exist without a core element designed to improve the world in which we live.

Social Brands

Beyond humanizing brands and social responsibilities, iGen expects brands to have personality. This is not the same notion as creating a "brand personality," which in essence delivers a position and voice for branded communication, but rather gives a brand an actual personality that consumers can identify with, connect with, and communicate with. If we assume that iGen requires interaction with a brand, then we must also assume brands can be interacted with. It is difficult to interact with a corporation, product, box, or brand message.

Giving a brand a personality requires more than a human face. The brand voice, presence, and overall experience must be anthropomorphized to the point where the brand may not even need a human face. This brand persona, prevalent in design, messaging, logos, etc., must permeate outbound communication to the extent that iGen has a platform from which to interact.

Take two examples: e-newsletter solutions Constant Contact and MailChimp. Both platforms deliver easy-to-customize e-newsletters that penetrate spam filters and make it easy for small businesses, nonprofits, and corporations alike to e-mail their constituents. Both are perfectly viable, similarly priced, and reliable products. Both deliver thought-leadership solutions such as webinars, marketing information, and demos.

Constant Contact's homepage is conservative, clearly small-business-focused, and prominently displays tools that will make marketing easier. Key words include "know your customers," and the site touts features, social media integration, and robust solutions. MailChimp's homepage features a large image of a chimp, and while it also touts features, it uses casual language such as "Guides for Everything" and "Need convincing?" and first-person positioning: "We do this" and "We do that." This playful personality permeates the product, including error messages that uses the word "shucks" and a chimp saying in a comic at the header, "Rocking it in my music vest, yo" (which links to a hilarious '80s-era YouTube video on the MailChimp feed about a product called Music Vest).

Which site appeals to iGen? The small-business solution or the helpful and playfully interactive small-business solution? Granted, iGen may have no need for e-newsletters at present, but MailChimp is clearly on the edge of a new type of branded interaction that digital natives will expect from their vendors and products.

Movember is another example of a cause with personality that is geared toward digital natives. The non-profit supports prostate cancer initiatives by raising money through brand ambassadors who grow mustaches in November. The brand is not only interactive but it also builds its entire fundraising model on being interactive. Therefore, its personality is such that the brand is very easy to interact with. The website is playful, kitschy, and provokes humorous response: an effective tool for creating awareness about a very serious cause.

Brand personalities need not be playful or humorous to be interactive, but it helps. Studies show that digital natives prefer ads that are "funny." This is likely because humor is the great equalizer. That said, iGen is likely to respond just as well to personalities that they can identify with even if they aren't humorous. One example is the "It Gets Better Project," a nonprofit that curates videos designed to empower young LGBT people against bullying. The project's supportive and interactive approach resulted in fifty thousand videos viewed more than fifty million times.

The key to an effective brand personality is to give the brand a personality: a humanized expression that is easy to relate to and interact with. The more distant, product-oriented, or detached a brand seems, the more difficult it is for iGen to interact with it. If a brand does everything else right for iGen, it will still fall on deaf ears if, ultimately, interaction is difficult.

Social Commerce

One of the more remarkable ideas Groupon helped to bring to the main stage was social commerce. They were one of the few innovators that went out of the gates of social media with a monetization structure. The idea that groups of people pay money through social media was nothing short of extraordinary; not even a year later, Zynga took over and proved that not only will people pay money through social media; *they will do it for things that don't exist in the physical world*. Even during the Great Recession, people were not afraid to buy virtual animals to put on their fictional farms or plunk down five real dollars for five fake dollars' worth of fake poker chips.

Social commerce has evolved in a short time to do to

pricing and inventory management what social media did to media: put it in the hands of the consumer. Successful online retailers will take note of what happens when commerce is socialized and influenced by the purchaser. iGen will spend in the same way they do everything else: socially. They will want to know what their friends are buying and from whom; what's more, they will want to be able to influence price, availability, and merchandise. Companies that are able to manage this inverted online retail model will thrive in the post-disrupted world.

When Things Go Wrong

In public relations, it has always been important to be ethical and transparent at all times, especially in a crisis when transparency seems like a liability and ethics aren't easily considered. However, exposure for unethical behavior has never been higher and further, neither have the stakes. Before the disruption, firms could recover from exposed poor ethical behavior with enough time and positive public relations.

Just like in all other brand communications, iGen in particular, but digital natives in general, will not accept communications to satisfy exposed bad ethics. They will require re-entry into the circle of trust that they may never grant, but that will require consistent and long-term action that demonstrates the unethical behavior was corrected.

Transparency and ethics in business have always been the hallmark of success, but now, those companies that have not operated this way are exposed. With iGen, there are no more secrets; the future of capitalism will be built upon interactive transparency with target audiences.

That said, things will inevitably go wrong. In those instances, companies need transparent, honest, and ethical crisis communication. iGen will not accept communication that "spins" or covers up the truth of what happened. They want the gory details, and beyond that, they want it quickly and with "next steps" to resolving the issue.

Who

TOMS Shoes

What Was Going On

Blake Mycoskie befriended children in Argentina who had no shoes and so started TOMS Shoes in 2006 with a "one-for-one movement" that would match every pair of shoes sold with a pair of shoes given to a child in need.

What They Did

Within one year, TOMS provided ten thousand pairs of shoes, and by 2010, TOMS donated one million shoes.

Why It Worked

TOMS is really a case in point on how brands can integrate purpose into their fabric. Giving a pair of shoes with each purchase isn't only cause marketing; it is the brand's very identity. Clearly this model resonated and catapulted the for-profit business into a recognized movement and powerful brand name.

Who

BP

What Was Going On

In 2002, British Petroleum rebranded itself as "Beyond Petroleum," a campaign that eventually became synonymous with green washing. This branding effort along with other global ad campaigns designed to position as BP working toward an environmental solution successfully put the brand in the "green" category by media outlets like the *Financial Times* and *Forbes*.

What They Did

What happened: During this green campaign, BP was operationally creating major environmental problems including a ruptured refinery that was found to have been caused by negligence, an Alaskan spill in 2006 in which they were found negligent, and in 2007 a series of violations in an offshore oil rig. However, it took the notorious 2010 oil spill in the Gulf for BP to drop the campaign.

Why It Didn't Work

The bottom line is that BP was disingenuously tapping an increasing trend of environmental consumerism. They have become the poster child for green washing and there was a shocking lack of transparency after the major Gulf of Mexico oil spill. iGen will not buy into these types of marketing tactics.

The Net Net

iGen loves to advocate for responsibile brands that impress them and publicly dismiss brands that don't.

Chapter Eight

"Hey, What's the Big Idea?" - The New Normal is Here

i Gen was born beginning in 1994. Their formative years took place during the massive communications disruption of the past decade. There is no other reality for those born on or around 2005. This is a generation born with consumer-driven capitalism at its core and altruism at its heart. Never before was there a generation so globally plugged in and so informed. The entirety of human knowledge and wisdom is instantaneously accessible. There are no geographical boundaries, and political boundaries are increasingly antiquated. This is the new normal.

So while, as marketers, we have to adapt our processes to access this new generation, it should be understood that iGen is already consuming and will quickly join Gen Y as a global majority. Traditional strategies and tactics certainly have a role, but unless they are geared for the specific collective behavior and sensitivities of iGen, then brands will quickly become obsolete.

This need not be a systemic organizational change but can rather be a change in thinking. Systems, processes, programs, and tactics will all organically change once organizations begin collectively thinking with the new generation in mind.

There is an unprecedented opportunity to directly reach a desirable target market with tremendous brand advocacy behavior. Never before have marketers had access to such a receptive and innovative market. However, with the opportunity comes a fundamental change. It requires risks that brands never had to take and concessions of messaging that were always controlled. The new environment is fast-paced, always in motion, and in constant shift. Brands need to be nimble, thick-skinned, and smart. Most importantly, brands need to be sincere.

iGen understands that brands have what they want and that without brands, they cannot make genuine and permanent change in their society. However, they have been conditioned not to trust brands, and they have been raised with limitless choices for brands. Given this environment, they will always choose the brands that speak to who they are, that make them proud of who they are. They will leave insincere or unplugged brands to their parents and choose the ones that earn their trust.

We are only now cresting the wave that is our new reality. Much of the path has been made clear by recent innovators, both new and disruptive brands as well as legacy brands that were wise to the new marketplace. Now that we are past this disruption, we can spot new and important trends that are around the corner. Technology may change dramatically by the year, but the intent will always be the same: efficiency on interaction. As long as brands, strategies, and programs are geared for that environment, then success will come easier.

The Mobile Appendage

In the middle of 2012, Nielsen reported that over 50 percent of Americans use smartphones, which, for the first time, outperformed "dumb" phones.[66] The Pew Internet Project announced around the same time that almost 90 percent of smartphone users check the Internet on their phones, nearly 70 percent do so every day, and 25 percent use the phone more than a computer.[67] *Forbes* recently noted that mobile website traffic has crossed the 50 percent threshold, indicating that the "addictive" nature of tablets is taking over the core functionality of computers.[68] When only focused on the youth, these numbers dramatically increase. Not only are landlines in rapid decline (and in some demographics not used at all), but so are computers. Since the introduction of the iPhone and the subsequent iPad, America has quickly adopted a new, highly efficient mobile addiction.

Smartphones and tablets have become our appendages. They are extensions of ourselves. We keep our financial information, personal information, photos, calendars, books, telephone, music, magazines, newspapers, social communities, games, maps, directories, shopping lists, coupons, weather reports, briefcases with business documents, cameras, recipes, televisions, catalogs, word processors and spreadsheets, credit cards and cash registers, and dictionaries on our person at all times. In many ways, our entire mundane life has been wrapped up and packaged into one easy-to-access device. We can check stocks, weather, updates on business docs, all while showing pictures of our kids and pets to people offline and online. We can listen to music, find directions, read the news, watch movies, and make phone calls. We can check prices, ask for advice, share documents, read books, and write restaurant reviews. There is very little in our everyday lives that cannot be managed by our mobile devices.

Many of us have become incredibly dependent upon these devices. We don't lose them because we notice within seconds if we have left them somewhere. We don't break them because they are always in our pockets or desktops. We have become so accustomed to the feel of a vibrating phone call or alert, researchers have even found a neurological disorder where our legs will feel "phantom" vibrations.[69]

Philosophically, they could be considered an extension of ourselves or perhaps of our identity. They are the gateway between the virtual world and the physical world that has increasingly thinning boundaries. They connect us to the infinite amounts of data that we reference every minute of every day. They also connect us with other people in ways we have never connected with before: instant access to location, activities, thoughts, conversations, and ideas; all of which used to be limited by geography, proximity, and time but which now have exponentially opened up, breaking down all those barriers of human connection.

And if this is the scenario *now*, what will it look like tomorrow? iGen is native to this. They grew up watching their parents communicate on small devices 24/7, reading books on tablets, and watching movies on smartphones. They grew up permanently connected and with a surrogate brain held in one's hand that did all of the daily activities humans do. It is their appendage, existentially linked to a virtual and simultaneously real world.

The mobile appendage means that we interact with the virtual world from the physical world, in real time and with an unlimited duration. We are permanently connected to the virtual world through a mobile and constantly interacting interface, and as technology improves, barriers to interaction will increasingly go away. Google Glass, Google's eywear that takes augmented reality to another level is an example of where we are heading. This is only the beginning. Technology is becoming so fast and efficient, it is no longer limited by the size of the device; it is limited by our own limitations with accessing the device.

Removing physical barriers to interacting with the Internet is the Holy Grail of technology. Eyewear aside, companies have been able to use sensors to track brain patterns enough to cause objects to move. This technology is so developed that there are currently toys on the market that literally utilize mind control to levitate objects. It is only a matter of time before we will be able to type, swipe, navigate, and communicate through the Internet using only our thoughts.

User interaction isn't the only part of the formula for interfacing with the Internet. Augmented Reality technology has made tremendous strides over the past few years. AR overlays digital information over the real world, using smartphones or cameras. An example might be looking into your computer monitor and having an animated face superimposed over yours. More high-tech examples include attaching virtual information on real-world objects through bar codes. There is technology in development that can translate languages in real time, and superimpose the translation over the physical object (such as a street sign). AR is allowing us to superimpose the virtual world over our own real world.

We have a dramatic future ahead as we continue to figure out how to seamlessly interface with the Internet and the digital world. While platforms, technologies, and websites will change, the ultimate direction is here to stay: we see the real world with digital eyes and interact in it with digital hands. This changes everything about how marketing works. The digital imprint of a brand and the physical imprint are equally important so communication must exist in harmony in both universes.

Reaching iGen's Infinite Touch Points

Once inside iGen's "circle of trust," you will be able to reach them anytime and anywhere. Their permanently connected mobile appendage makes them efficient recipients of information and their online footprints make them effective brand advocates. Following are some tactics that can help to reach iGen on any of their infinite touch points.

Do . . .

- Utilize monitoring tools to find conversations and brand mentions online and respond specifically to solve a problem, but not to promote one's self, direct to a product, or market.

- Respond immediately and professionally to anyone who asks a question or brings up a problem online.

- Provide alternative venues for interaction besides traditional channels such as TV, radio, print, website, and make those channels accessible and active, such as social media, mobile site, SMS, etc.

- Create a mobile app that solves a specific problem. It is not enough to have a mobile version of a website as an app; the app must serve a specific purpose and fulfill a need.

Don't . . .

- Pretend you are a consumer in order to gain trust with other consumers.

- Ignore direct questions or problems presented to your brand online.

- Provide a canned message to a personal inquiry online.

- Ignore social media.

Accessing iGen's Omnipresent Impulse Zone

Because iGen is permanently connected, they can potentially have a point of sale anywhere. Brands can bypass the convoluted marketing funnel and create an impulse zone wherever there is a point of purchase. To do this online, marketers must fuse the online and offline worlds right where iGen makes purchases, such as through geo-location coupon services, real-world POS locations, etc.

Do . . .

- Find brick-and-mortar retail partners that appeal to your target audience and provide access to your product digitally there, through bar codes, signage, handouts, or other materials that direct consumers to your online properties.

- Utilize location-based services such as LivingSocial and Groupon to leverage the digital impulse zone for your product and service.

- Provide incentives for customers to check in and interact digitally when in your brand's physical location.

- Develop partnerships with existing distribution channels to have a gateway online, such as mailers with shipped product, newsletters, etc.

Don't . . .

- Treat social media sites as static web pages with no interaction or incentive to return.

- Ignore the physical world and focus entirely online.

- Ignore the online world and focus entirely offline.

- Send communication to clients or prospects without including both offline and online communication channels.

Finding Influencers

iGen listens to iGen because they have been conditioned to not trust marketing. In order to effectively reach them, then, brands must communicate through trustworthy influencers who then communicate to consumers. Finding influencers can be a tricky business because, unlike spokespeople, they have a mouthpiece of their own and no obligation to be consistent with controlled brand messaging.

Do . . .

- Carefully research an audience to find out what influencers have the most impact on them before approaching an influencer.

- Choose an influencer who is closely aligned with the brand and whose typical communication style fits in comfortably with the brand's.

- Be transparent that you are partnering with a brand advocate.

- Choose influencers who are influential both in the offline and online space.

Don't . . .

- Attempt to control what the influencer can or cannot say.

- Secretly compensate an influencer for brand advocacy.

- Choose influencers based solely upon the size of their online following without also checking out the level of engagement of that following.

- Pretend to be an influencer among a peer audience.

Curating Content

A very effective way to reach iGen is to become a source for important information that iGen is actively searching for. This can be achieved by carefully curating content so that no other source can provide the same level of information iGen needs on a particular topic that is relevant to your brand.

Do . . .

- Curate content from established and respectable experts in your topic's field.

- Be transparent about compensation on contributed content from experts.

- Create editorial calendars for writers and develop a news center.

- Build the perception as a leader of relevant news in the field and as an expert source

Don't . . .

- Promote products and services as "news."

- Utilize curated space for advertisements or advertorials.

- Censor or block editorial content.

- Be misleading or unethical with editing and publishing content.

Aligning with Personal Brands

When iGen finds a brand that they personally identify with, they are happy to serve as brand advocates. One way to reach iGen is to align a brand with the audience's personal brand. This can be done by positioning a brand as a lifestyle and then communicating that lifestyle to iGen.

Do . . .

- Know the lifestyle habits of your target audience.

- Create programs and communication consistent with that lifestyle.

- Invite the target audience to participate with the brand through interactive programs such as contests, videos, or social media interaction.

- Develop content that your target audience would naturally share and re-share, whether because of humor, brand alignment, or connection with a lifestyle.

Don't . . .

- Be disingenuous or shallow, pretend to be something a brand is not.

- Target the right audience with the wrong lifestyle.

- Target the wrong audience with the right lifestyle.

- Expect publicity stunts to have staying power.

Having a Purpose

One of the most effective ways of creating a brand that iGen will be attracted to and become a brand advocate for is to create a brand with a purpose. iGen naturally supports brands that have social responsibility woven into their fabric.

Do . . .

- Support a cause that naturally fits with the brand personality.

- Create programs that include all levels of the organization beyond just marketing, including operations, human resources, distribution, etc.

- Create a brand that has a distinct purpose in society and that, if absent, would detract from society.

- Communicate a brand's social purpose through action, not only through messages.

Don't . . .

- Utilize shallow cause marketing tactics to appear to be socially responsible.

- Be unethical about cause marketing.

- Ignore cause marketing and social responsibility.

- Create cause marketing programs without knowing your brand's social purpose.

The Net Net

Digital natives in general and iGen in particular present marketers and brands with both the largest opportunity for direct consumer interaction and the largest barrier in which to do so. This is a generation that knows before we do, has no incentive or requirement to hear our messaging, and relies upon unprecedented amounts of data that is processed inconceivably fast in order to make the most informed decisions of any generation to date. Our challenge as marketers is not only understanding how to reach iGen, but also how to co-exist with them. For the first time in our industry's history, we are in an environment where we must earn the privilege to communicate to our audiences.

Our role is a humble one. We no longer have the luxury of mass communication that, when splattered against the wall, reaches enough people to do the job. No one is even looking at the wall now. So it is time to go into the trenches, live with our audience, and become a trusted part of their network. We need to be the mailman the neighborhood sees every day, the family on the block that always delivers cookies on Saturday afternoons, or the lovable business owner who sometimes gives sweets to the neighborhood kids for free.

iGen doesn't demand much of us. They like our products and services and will happily tell their friends. They just don't want to be hammered on, lied to, or treated like cattle. They are individuals, but unlike the generations before them, they are pragmatic individuals. They understand that the welfare of the herd is equal to the welfare of the individual, and so they put a special sort of trust in the groups they claim allegiance to. We only get one chance to be a part of the group. There are too many opportunities and options now; iGen will reject us and never look back if we violate their trust. And if we never attempt to join their group in the first place, they have no use for us if they even see us.

It is difficult to say if this global social disruption happened the moment Steve Jobs unveiled the iPad on that fateful day in April, 2010. True, these trends were on an upswing for nearly ten years. One could even point to the invention of Google, the tool that democratized the Internet by only showing relevant results based upon what users thought relevant. Or maybe eBay, the first global garage sale. Or Amazon, where user reviews take precedent over the experts. Or perhaps it was Napster, which single-handedly inverted the entire music industry. Maybe it was the invention of wireless technology, or high-speed Internet, or 3G cellular networks. It could have been Palm's Treo or BlackBerry. Facebook. Twitter. We may never know precisely where the epicenter was. Most likely, it was like all things human, a perfect storm of intelligence converging all at once to create a technological Renaissance unlike anything we have ever seen.

But as we stand in the shadow of this Renaissance, it is easy to forget that iGen knows no other world. This is their normal. We are not in a position to tell them how to behave as consumers. They will simply consume. It is up to us to figure out how they do so.

As I finished this book, so much has changed that already I must go back and update and edit an incredible amount of material. By the time the book is on the shelves, there will be passages that will be out of date and perhaps entirely antiquated. Our world now moves too fast for books, even if some of us still do read them. Clearly the challenge is beyond only content . . . it is a much larger scope. Our challenge is to understand the very infrastructure of our new world, for the fleeting pages of content are impermanent, but our new world-view is not.

The net net is this: We must now listen in order to be heard.

Notes

1. Ethan Lyon, "Examining Generation Z: Stats, Demographics, Segments, Predictions," *Sparxoo*, February 23, 2012, accessed January 31, 2012, http://www.sparxoo.com/2010/02/23/examining-generation-z-stats-demographics-segments-predictions/.

2. *Ibid.*

3. *Ibid.*

4. Tamar Lewin, "Screen Time Higher Than Ever for Children," *New York Times*, October 25, 2011, accessed February 6, 2012, http://www.nytimes.com/2011/10/25/us/screen-time-higher-than-ever-for-children-study-finds.html?_r=1.

5. Terracarmichael, "Bell Swiping TV Like iPhone," YouTube, October 6, 2012, accessed February 6, 2012, http://www.youtube.com/watch?v=qGO8zgqNEbA.

6. *Ibid.*

7. Mike Elgan, "Why iPad Is the 'Children's Toy of the Year'," *Computerworld*, March 6, 2010, accessed February 21, 2012, http://www.computerworld.com/s/article/9166878/Mike_Elgan_Why_iPad_is_the_Children_s_Toy_of_the_Year_.

8. "Zero to Eight: Children's Media Use in America," *Common*

Sense Media, October 25, 2011, accessed January 31, 2012, http://www.commonsensemedia.org/research/zero-eight-childrens-media-use-america/key-finding-1%3A-young-children-use-digital-media-frequently.

9. *Ibid.*

10. Brian X. Chen, "Flops Pile Up in the Tablet Market," *New York Times*, December 7, 2011, accessed February 21, 2012, https://www.evernote.com/Home.action#b=cc82c712-3f87-474a-a6eb-b3846ba47d39&x=nytimes&n=36370c8c-e000-4dd9-8a71-7ae0615960fe.

11. *Ibid.*

12. Matthew Ingram, "Mary Meeker: Mobile Internet Will Soon Overtake Fixed Internet," *GigaOM*, April 12, 2012, accessed February 21, 2012, http://gigaom.com/2010/04/12/mary-meeker-mobile-internet-will-soon-overtake-fixed-internet/.

13. *Ibid.*

14. Daryl Choy, "What Exactly Is Touchpoint?" *Customer Think*, June 12, 2008, accessed February 16, 2012, http://www.customerthink.com/blog/what_exactly_touchpoint.

15. Eric Clemons, "Why Advertising Is Failing on the Internet," *TechCrunch*, March 22, 2009, http://techcrunch.com/2009/03/22/why-advertising-is-failing-on-the-internet/.

16. Katerina-Eva Matsa, Tom Rosenstiel, and Paul Moore, "Magazines: A Shake-Out for News Weeklies," State of the News Media 2011, http://stateofthemedia.org/2011/magazines-essay/.

17. Meghan Peters, "Internet Surpasses Television as Main News Source for Young Adults," *Mashable*, January 4, 2011, accessed February 4, 2012, http://mashable.com/2011/01/04/internet-surpasses-television-as-main-news-source-for-young-adults-study/.

18. Adam Cohen, with Gargi Patel, "The New Marketing Funnel," *Social Media Today*, August 13, 2009, http://socialmediatoday.com/index.php?q=SMC/116164.

19. Brian Solis, The End of Business as Usual: Rewire the Way You Work to Succeed in the Consumer Revolution. (Hoboken, NJ: John Wiley & Sons, 2012).

20. Will Palley, "With Upward Spiral, Starbucks' Schultz Becomes Job-Creation Advocate," J W T AnxietyIndex, August 29, 2011, http://anxietyindex.com/2011/08/with-upward-spiral-starbucks-schultz-becomes-job-creation-advocate/.

21. Paula Forbes, "Taco Bell Ad: Thank You for Suing Us," *Eater*, January 28, 2011, http://eater.com/archives/2011/01/28/taco-bell-ad-thanks-firm-for-law-suit.php.

22. "Rite Aid Reaches $1.38 by Improving Weakest Stores, Cutting Dead Weight," *Seeking Alpha*, October 10, 2011, http://seekingalpha.com/article/298683-rite-aid-reaches-1-38-by-improving-weakest-stores-cutting-dead-weight.

23. "Walgreens February Sales Increase 1.5 Percent," press release, Walgreens, March 5, 2012, http://news.walgreens.com/article_display.cfm?article_id=5556.

24. "Retailer Presentation," *Front-End Focus*, https://www.google.com/url?sa=t&rct=j&q=&esrc=s&source=web&cd=2&cad=rja&ved=0CDcQFjAB&url=http%3A%2F%2Fwww.frontendfocus.com%2Fdocuments%2Fpublications%2FFront-End%2520Focus%2520Overall%2520Study.pdf&ei=rGTsUK3UMMmQiAKXrIDACw&usg=AFQjCNEAH9DCTqtGx24hL_k0ajf1Ps0Hkg.

25. Bill Cromwell, "Magazine Newsstand Sales Slide Again," *Media Life Magazine*, February 7, 2012, http://www.medialifemagazine.com/artman2/publish/Magazines_22/Magazine-newsstand-sales-slide-again.asp.

26. Jeffrey G. Stern, "Confectionary Sales Up despite Global Downturn," Jeffrey G. Stern, August 30, 2011, http://jeffreygstern.com/chocolate-trends/confectionery-sales-up-despite-global-downturn/.

27. Dany, "Search Engine Optimisation (SEO): How and When Did SEO Begin?" *Terranet*, July 12, 2010, http://terranet.md/blog/viral-seo/search-engine-optimisation-seo-how-and-when-did-it-all-begin/.

28. Kelly Reeves, "Study Gives Insight into Content Discovery Trends across the Web's Leading Publishers," *Outbrain*, April 14, 2011, http://blog.outbrain.com/2011/04/outbrain-

content-discovery-report.html.

29. Todd Wasserman, "Facebook to Hit 1 Billion User Mark in August," *Mashable,* January 12, 2012, http://mashable.com/2012/01/12/facebook-1-billion-users/.

30. "Global Mobile Statistics 2012 Home: All the Latest Stats on Mobile Web, Apps, Marketing, Advertising, Subscribers, and Trends," *MobiThinking,* accessed January 2, 2013, http://mobithinking.com/mobile-marketing-tools/latest-mobile-stats.

31. "Generation Z - The Future Employee," Boomer Match to Business, accessed January 2, 2013, http://www.bm2b.ca/blog-reader/items/generation-z.html.

32. "Live Births and Birth Rates, by Year," *Infoplease,* 2007, http://www.infoplease.com/ipa/A0005067.html.

33. AJ Arora, "Almost Three: A Brief History of Foursquare Time (And a Look at Its Future)," *TechCrunch,* February 26, 2012, http://techcrunch.com/2012/02/26/a-brief-history-of-foursquare/.

34. Mark Hachman, Mark. "Facebook Launches 'Places' with FourSquare, Gowalla," *PCMAG,* August 18, 2010. , http://www.pcmag.com/article2/0,2817,2368002,00.asp.

35. Pamela Vaughan, Pamela. "Facebook Kills Places, Foursquare and Gowalla Rejoice," *HubSpot,* August 24, 2011, http://blog.hubspot.com/blog/tabid/6307/bid/23555/Facebook-Kills-Places-Foursquare-and-Gowalla-Rejoice.aspx.

36. Sarah Kessler, "Checking In Is the Least Popular Smartphone Activity," Mashable, September 6, 2011, http://mashable.com/2011/09/06/location-based-services-unpopular/.

37. Britney Fitzgerald, "Americans Addicted To Checking Smartphones, Would 'Panic' If They Lost Device (STUDY)," *The Huffington Post,* June 21, 2012, http://www.huffingtonpost.com/2012/06/21/americans-are-addicted-to-smartphones_n_1615293.html.

38. "2011: The Year the Check-In Died," *ReadWrite,* April 12, 2011, http://www.readwriteweb.com/archives/2011_the_year_the_check-in_died.php.

39. "Did iTunes Kill the Record Store?" *RoughDrafted,* March 2, 2007, http://www.roughlydrafted.com/RD/RDM.Tech.Q1.07/1C726ADF-0ED1-42D0-93D9-4FA4E698E94A.html.

40. Christine Maxwell, ed., "Global Trends that Will Impact

Universal Access to Information Resources," ISOC, July 15, 2000, http://www.isoc.org/isoc/unesco-paper.shtml.

41. "Technology May Be Altering How Brains Work," *Associated Press, NBCNEWS.com*, December 3, 2008, http://www.msnbc.msn.com/id/28035543/ns/health-behavior/t/technology-may-be-altering-how-brains-work/#.T4NEtZpSQ5g.

42. Maureen Cavanaugh and Natalie Walsh, "How Technology Is Changing Our Brain," *KPBS*, August 10, 2009, http://www.kpbs.org/news/2009/apr/22/how-technology-changing-our-brain/.

43. Andrew Bendelow, "How to Teach the Millennial Learner? Critically," *Wikiness*, November 14, 2010,. http://thewikiness.blogspot.com/2010/11/how-to-teach-millennial-learner.html.

44. "Comedian Pete Holmes on Why Google Is Ruining Our Lives—Interesting Point" *Chive*, October 20, 2011,. http://thechive.com/2011/10/20/comedian-pete-holmes-on-why-google-is-ruining-our-lives-interesting-point-video/.

45. Stefanie Olsen, "Intelligence in the Internet Age," *CNET*, September 19, 2005, http://news.cnet.com/Intelligence-in-the-Internet-age---page-2/2100-11395_3-5869719-2.html?tag=mncol.

46. Hannah Richardson, "Students Only Have '10-Minute Attention Span,'" *BBC News*, January 12, 2010, http://news.bbc.co.uk/2/hi/uk_news/education/8449307.stm.

47. "Connected Devices Become Key to Content Consumption," Marketer, February 17, 2012, http://www.emarketer.com/Article.aspx?R=1008849.

48. "Yume and IPG Media Lab Release Findings on Effectiveness of Online and Televised Video Advertising," http://www.yumenetworks.com/content/yume-and-ipg-media-lab-release-findings-effectiveness-online-and-televised-video-advertising.

49. Anna Marevska, "The Mommy Blog Phenomenon," *Cision Navigator*, October 29, 2009. , http://navigator.cision.com/The_Mommy_Blog_Phenomenon.aspx.

50. Stephanie Azzarone, "De-Dooce This: What Makes a

'Mommy Blog' Successful?" *Mom Market Trends*, accessed March 2, 2011, http://www.childsplaypr.com/blog/de-dooce-this-what-makes-a-mommy-blog-successful/http://mommarkettrends.com/tag/mommy-bloggers/.

51. Ed Keller & Brad Fay, *The Face-to-Face Book*, 2010.

52. "Introducing Generation C: Americans 18--34 Are the Most Connected," *Nielsen Wire*, accessed February 23, 2012, http://blog.nielsen.com/nielsenwire/online_mobile/introducing-generation-c/.

53. Nellie Andreeva, "Full 2011--2012 TV Season Series Rankings," *Deadline Hollywood*, May 24, 2012, http://www.deadline.com/2012/05/full-2011-2012-tv-season-series-rankings/.

54. Bill Carter, "For Fox's Rivals, 'American Idol' Remains a 'Schoolyard Bully,'" *The New York Times*, February 20, 2007, http://www.nytimes.com/2007/02/20/arts/television/20idol.html?_r=2.

55. Digital Music News, 2012, http://www.digitalmusicnews.com/.

56. Ben Sisario, "Digital Notes: After Steep Declines, Music Sales in 2011 Held Steady," Media Briefing, March 26, 2012, http://www.themediabriefing.com/article/2012-03-26/digital-notes-after-steep-declines-music-sales-in-2011-held-steady.

57. Greg Stuart, "You Can't Avoid Ad Avoidance," *Adweek*, September 8, 2008, http://www.adweek.com/news/advertising-branding/you-cant-avoid-ad-avoidance-96852.

58. William A. Hachten, The Troubles of Journalism: A Critical Look at What's Right and Wrong with the Press. (New York: Taylor & Francis, 2005), accessed December 20, 2012, http://books.google.com/books?id=_mXTyRtjLYMC.

59. Claire Suddath, "25 Things I Didn't Want to Know about You," *Time*, February 5, 2009. http://www.time.com/time/arts/article/0,8599,1877187,00.html.

60. Brian Solis, "The 6 Pillars of Social Commerce: Understanding the Psychology of Engagement," *Fast Company*, March 19, 2012, http://www.fastcompany.com/1825374/the-6-pillars-of-social-commerce-understanding-the-psychology-of-engagement.

61. GoodPurpose, Edelman, http://purpose.edelman.com/.

62. AMP Agency, "The Millennial Generation: Pro-Social and Empowered to Change the World," *GreenBook*, http://www.greenbook.org/marketing-research.cfm/millennial-cause-study.

63. Louise Jack, "Your Next Marketing Challenge: Gen Z," *Fast Company*, September 7, 2012, accessed September 10, 2012, http://www.fastcocreate.com/1681549/your-next-marketing-challenge-gen-z.

64. Aman Singh, "A New Study Reveals a Startling Fact about How the Public Feels about CSR," *Forbes*, November 18, 2010, http://www.forbes.com/sites/csr/2010/11/18/a-new-study-reveals-a-startling-fact-about-how-the-public-feels-about-csr/.

65. *TriplePundit,* http://www.triplepundit.com/.

66. Enid Burns, "Half of Americans Own Smartphones, Use It to Read News," *RedOrbit*, October 1, 2012, http://www.redorbit.com/news/technology/1112704426/americans-smartphones-news-100112/.

67. Suzanne Choney, "Internet Making Our Brains Different, Not Dumb,." *NBCNEWS.com*, February 19, 2010, http://www.msnbc.msn.com/id/35464896/ns/technology_and_science-tech_and_gadgets/t/internet-making-our-brains-different-not-dumb/#.UOxvGYnjm44.

68. Anthony Wing Kosner,. "Tablets Will Take Over Sooner than You Think: Five Telling Trends," *Forbes*, March 4, 2012, http://www.forbes.com/sites/anthonykosner/2012/03/04/tablets-will-take-over-sooner-than-you-think-five-telling-trends/.

69. Angela Haupt, "Good Vibrations? Bad? None at All?" *USAToday,* June 12, 2007, http://usatoday30.usatoday.com/news/health/2007-06-12-cellphones_N.htm.

CPSIA information can be obtained at www.ICGtesting.com
Printed in the USA
BVOW04*1818030414

349583BV00001B/2/P